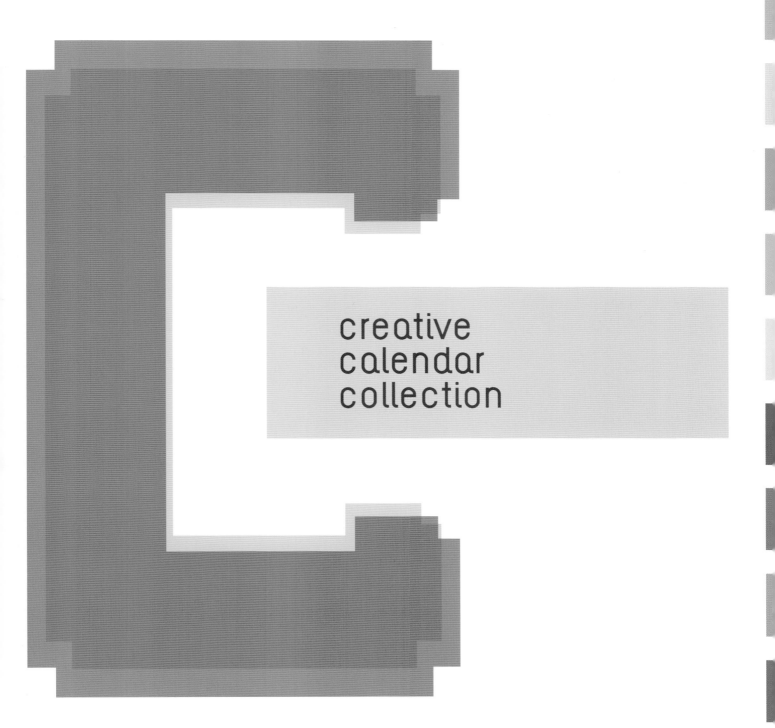

creative
calendar
collection

LINKS

a calendar is a tool that helps us not to lose sight of our commitments and daily activities. calendars are a system of timekeeping that defines the beginning, length, and divisions of the year in way of tables showing the months, weeks, and days in at least one specific year. calendars play an imperative role in our lives and define us by our tastes and styles. they are, like many of our personal belongings, an extension of our egos. latest advancements in technology have made it possible for us to incorporate our schedules and events into the calendars available in a virtual form in our mobile devices and computers, but nothing beats the experience of owning a conventional calendar. there are many who prefer to own and use calendars that are physically present which they can touch and feel, an experience that cannot be replicated by modern technology.

today, calendars are not just tools that tell you what day or month it is, but serve a much more subtle role in our lives. a well-designed and aesthetically pleasing calendar can alter the visual aspect of a room and can even be a subject around which casual conversations can revolve. calendars can also set trends, convey messages, portray design elements and most importantly, make a statement. knowing how important calendars are in our lives, basheer graphic books presents this book, creative calendar collection, a collection of designer calendars that have been especially designed to cater to a wide range of styles and personal preferences.

introduction

creative calendar collection presents some of the most avant-garde calendar designs from across the globe, featuring designs that range from the highly unusual to the downright bizarre. the book began as a quest to explore the far-reaches of calendar design, the limits of what is aesthetically and conceptually possible. the result is an extraordinary range of calendar designs contributed by various designers and studios such as kenji yano, masaaki kimura, the hong kong polytechnic university, "sonner, vallee u. partner", massachusetts college of art and design and many more. these designs include calendars that are ring bound; that can be folded into cubes; that come in highly configurable cut-out sheets; that resemble measuring tapes, to name but a few.

Wish You Were Here Calendar

The 'Wish You Were Here' A3 sized, spiral bound, ready-to-mount wall calendar 2010 was produced to collect together artwork by Ben the Illustrator, and as a product, to bring colour into the home. It was printed using eco-friendly Simitri digital inks on FSC mixed recycled paper. The calendar includes tips or ideas for certain days in the year, for example 'Get some fresh air' as Springtime begins and 'Make a banana, coconut and pineapple smoothie' in the middle of Summer. Each piece of artwork was created by Ben the Illustrator in Adobe Illustrator, guaranteeing perfect bold colours.

WYWH is a homewares brand based in the UK managed by Fiona O'Brien with all art prints and products designed by her husband Ben O'Brien (Ben the Illustrator).

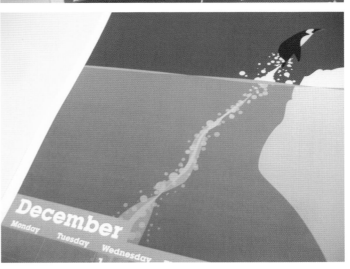

mono.gramm

www.mono-gramm.com

mono.gramm Spring/Summer 2010

The mono.Calender is a promotional item to thank friends and supporters for their help during the year. It is sent out as an A2 poster for free at the end of each year. A joint effort by mono.gramm, mono.graphie and mono.kultur.

mono.Calender 2009:
Photography: Kai von Rabenau
Design: Jessica Bentele

mono.Calender 2010:
Photography: Kai von Rabenau
Hair & Make-up: Julie Skok
Model: Nicole / Nine Daughters and a Stereo
Design: Jessica Bentele

www.mono-gramm.com

mono.Calender 2009:
Photography: Kai von Rabenau
Design: Jessica Bentele

mono.Calender 2010:
Photography: Kai von Rabenau
Hair & Make-up: Julie Skok
Model: Nicole / Nine Daughters and a Stereo
Design: Jessica Bentele

Mono Calender "Baltic Sea" 2009 / "mono.gramm Spring/Summer" 2010

The mono.Calender is a promotional item to thank friends and supporters for their help during the year. It is sent out as an A2 poster for free at the end of each year. A joint effort by mono.gramm, mono.graphie and mono.kultur.

niels kjeldsen design

www.niels-kjeldsen.dk

Corian Calendar

The design is a calendar made for the table. The user is in daily contact with the unique Corian material and can, by using the calendar, experience Corian´s luxurious surface, weight and high quality. All the new Corian colours are represented by the month-pieces. The calendar is composed of 12 Month-pieces in different colours, 2 Date-cubes in white and a solid base in black. The date is adjusted by turning the cubes around, and the month is changed by placing the relevant month in front of the date-cubes. Because the days are not named in the calendar, it can be used forever. The name 'Rainbow' reflects the shape of the base and the colours which move along its arc.

Dimensions: 312 x 85 x 120 mm

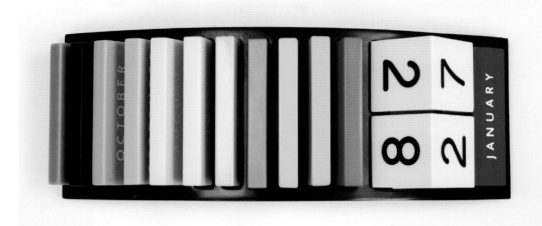

silnt
www.silnt.com

Art Director/Designer: ʃelix ng

The first of its series, Calendar Two Thousand and Nine is printed on 130 gsm New Raglin Recycled Paper and set in Mercury Display Type by Hoefler and Frere-Jones. Originally made for the designer's personal use, the calendar's unorthodox vertical format is ideal for marking project schedules and counting down to deadlines.

Dimensions: 841 x 271 mm

www.silnt.com

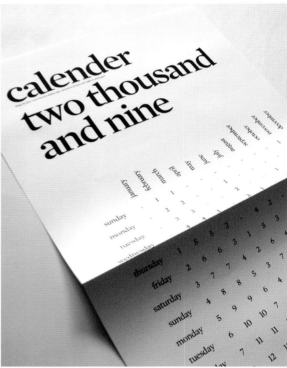

Calendar Two Thousand and Nine (black)

Maarten Janssens Calender

A calendar to kickstart 2010, this well-dressed time-manager will tell you what day fits a date and if the moon is full or new. Small enough not to consume necessary space on your desk and big enough for you to keep your eye on the ball: planning! Don't ask it why you only need a precision-knife and a bit of time, he doesn't have a glue.

Designer: Maarten Janssens

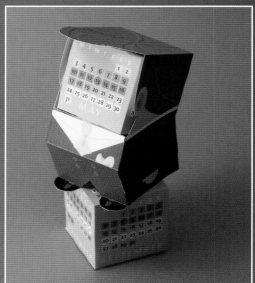
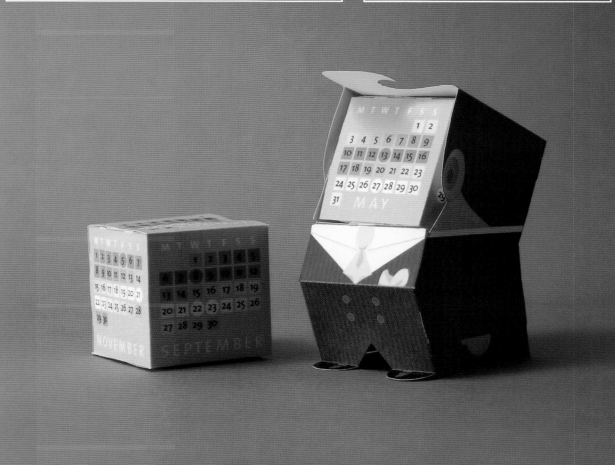

Cycles & Seasons 2009 Calendar Poster Set

Matt W. Moore is the founder of MWM Graphics, a design and illustration studio based in Portland, Maine. Matt works across disciplines, from colorful illustrations in his signature "Vectorfunk" style, to freeform watercolor paintings, and massive aerosol murals. MWM exhibits his artwork in galleries all around the world.

Dimensions: 18" x 12"

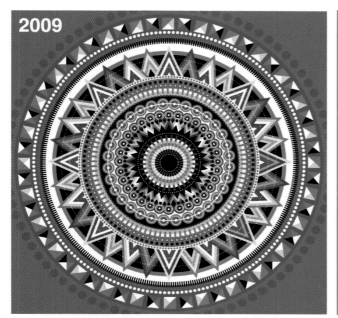
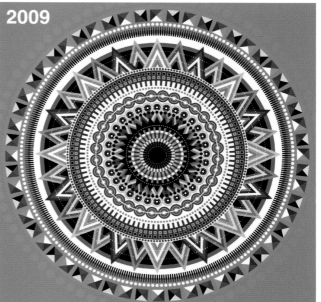
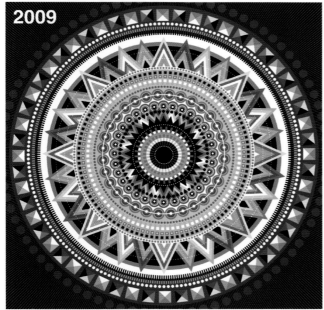
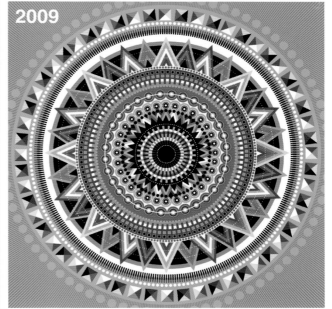

October						
S	M	T	W	T	F	S
				1	2	3
4	5	6	7	8	9	10
11	12	13	14	15	16	17
18	19	20	21	22	23	24
25	26	27	28	29	30	31

November						
S	M	T	W	T	F	S
1	2	3	4	5	6	7
8	9	10	11	12	13	14
15	16	17	18	19	20	21
22	23	24	25	26	27	28
29	30					

December						
S	M	T	W	T	F	S
		1	2	3	4	5
6	7	8	9	10	11	12
13	14	15	16	17	18	19
20	21	22	23	24	25	26
27	28	29	30	31		

April						
S	M	T	W	T	F	S
			1	2	3	4
5	6	7	8	9	10	11
12	13	14	15	16	17	18
19	20	21	22	23	24	25
26	27	28	29	30		

May						
S	M	T	W	T	F	S
					1	2
3	4	5	6	7	8	9
10	11	12	13	14	15	16
17	18	19	20	21	22	23
24	25	26	27	28	29	30
31						

June						
S	M	T	W	T	F	S
	1	2	3	4	5	6
7	8	9	10	11	12	13
14	15	16	17	18	19	20
21	22	23	24	25	26	27
28	29	30				

www.seesawdesigns.blogspot.com

2010 Letterpress Calendar

This calendar was inspired by nature and a love for classic modern shapes. The result is a playful exploration of form and color. The limited-edition wall calendar includes four designs, each with 3 months per page. Each piece was letterpress printed on Crane's Lettra 100% cotton paper using our antique Kluge printing press. The design emphasizes use after the year is over: trim off the dates, and keep the four pieces as prints.

Dimensions: 7.25"x11.5"

Designed By : Nick DuPey

Young Monster 2010 Calendars

Young Monster is an art collective based out of Chattanooga, TN, specializing in design and illustration. They provide unique, unflinching design solutions for all - from gig and event posters to branding and logo development to full-on marketing campaigns. With a core group of three graphic designers, a writer/clothing designer, and a rotating cast of additional friends and creatives, a fresh style is guaranteed for every project.

Dimensions: 17.5 x 21.5

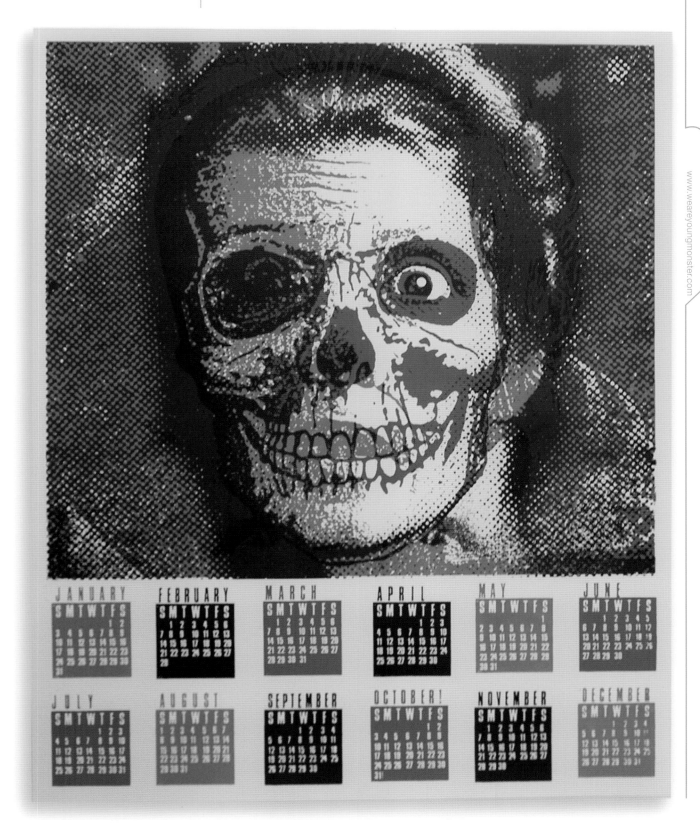

www.catsletnothingdarkentheirroar.com

For five years Cats Let Nothing Darken Their Roar Calendar has introduced new, odd, and strange phrases every month. The calendar is printed in four colours on matt paper, and comes with signature black ribbon binding. In 2010, to celebrate its 5th anniversary, it was available in a special large 50 x 70 cm size as well as in its standard A3 format, each in a numbered edition of 500.

Behind all these is Noa Bembibre (www.noabembibre.com) a Helsinki-based designer working in art direction and graphic design.

CATS LET NOTHING DARKEN THEIR ROAR

NINJA BUNNIES RUN NEARBY

FEDERAL BROOMS JUMP IF NECESSARY

TWO MATS ONE BIRCH

MANY PRIME NUMBERS LOVE FOREVER

AUTOMATIC YOLK

JUST EAT DINNER

JUNIOR PLUTO, MEET THE SKY

THE AUSTERE GLASS NEEDS LUSTER

SEPARATELY I REMEMBER

OCTAGON, BE NICER

NOTHING LIKE LITTLE VERA TO MAKE THINGS BETTER

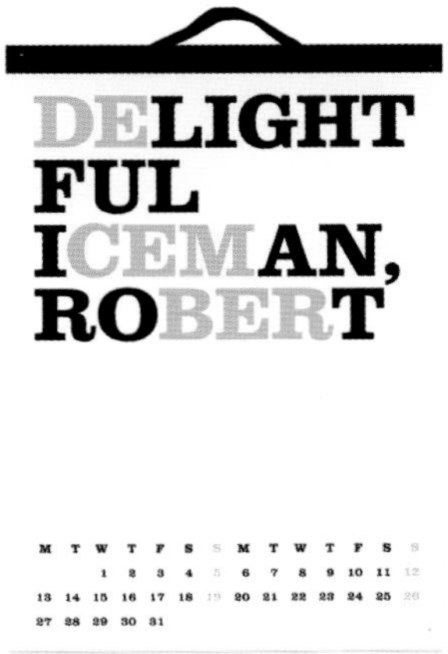

DELIGHTFUL ICEMAN, ROBERT

(Calendar 2009): Cross-section of Time

Client: Zwaan Printmedia
Designer: Ontwerphaven, Suzanne Hertogs

This 16-meter long artwork is an excursion through time and space to the most distant parts of the universe. A cross-section of the cosmos (through both live and dead matter) with our territory somewhere in the middle with its recognizable progress and history.

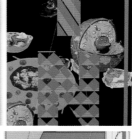

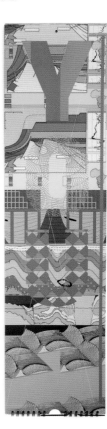

www.ontwerphaven.nl

Client: Ando bv, The Hague
Designer: Ontwerphaven, Suzanne Hertogs

(Agenda Calendar 2009): Verstand op Nul, Blik op Oneindig

The original title of the Dutch agenda "Verstand op Nul, Blik op Oneindig" (mind set on zero, vision to infinity) is a saying that means: Don't think - just do it. It is based on the assumption that if you don't think you can be very creative and do things you usually wouldn't do. This versatile calendar features an interior usually used as packaging paper. It is a gift of the agency to communicate its activities and the possibilities offered by good design.

Crispin Finn Year Planners 09

Of all the ugly office stationary products that one has to use on a daily basis, the year planner is a key offender. The intention behind this calendar was the creation of a beautiful year planner that made looking at one for a whole year a pleasure rather than a pain. The designers sought to create a product that had the same qualities of stationery made in the 1940s & 50s when items had an elegance and aesthetic clarity which served, rather than hindered, their practical role in everyday life. They also upheld the democratic design mantra that good design should be available to everyone. Embossed 2-color hand pulled screenprint on 120gsm 100% recycled white colorset. Each planner comes folded and sealed in a screenprinted brown craft bag.

Dimensions: 1000 x 700mm

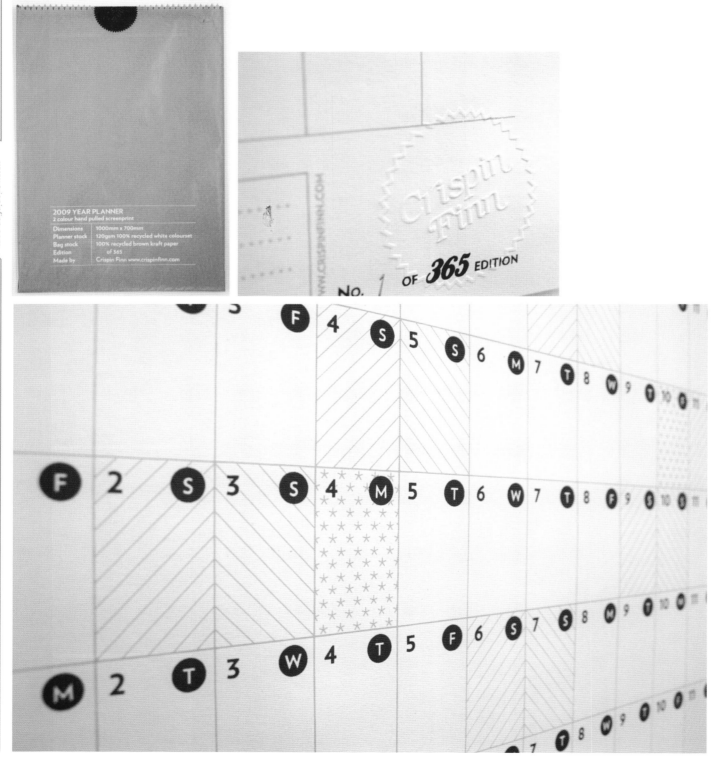

2009 YEAR PLANNER
2 colour hand pulled screenprint

Dimensions	1000mm x 700mm
Planner stock	120gsm 100% recycled white colourset
Bag stock	100% recycled brown kraft paper
Edition	of 365
Made by	Crispin Finn www.crispinfinn.com

No. 1 OF 365 EDITION

Crispin Finn Year Planners 10

Dimensions: 1000 x 700mm

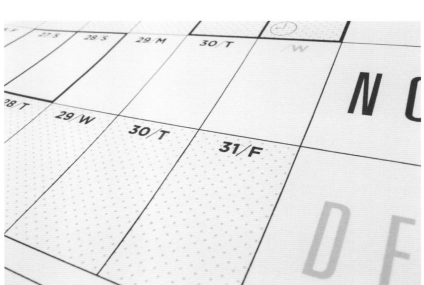

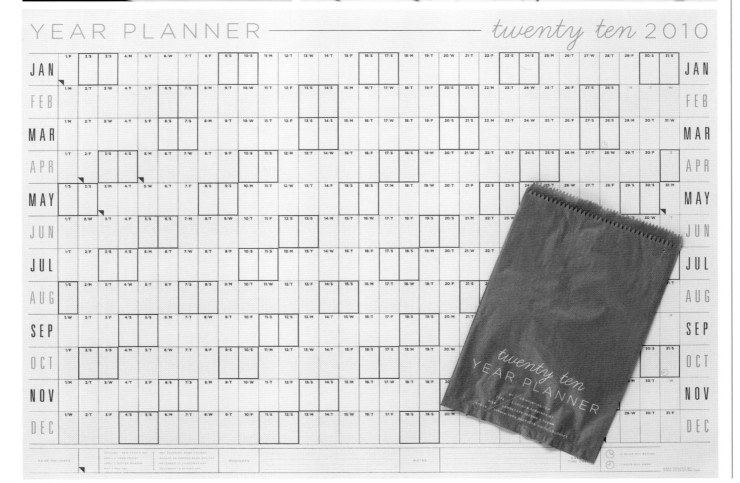

gagatree

www.gagatree.com

Calendar 2010

Creative juices overflow when least expected and yes, the bath is always a favourite. This calendar was created as a reminder of the passion the designers had for great design and the immensely popular products they had created and retailed over the year. No one foams the imagination like we do!

Creative Director: Lester Lim
Designer: Yang Qiao'E
Illustrator: Sam Har
Graphic Designer: Lee Ley Teng

mirit wissotzky

Calendar 2005

A project realized during second year studies at the Bezalel academy of art and design, Jerusalem. As time and days are a dazed idea, for each one of us special days or ordinary days, or even days to forget, get different meanings and expressions. Each day has his characteristics, there is no one identical to another.

There were only two limitations given: the format 28x28 and the use of black and white only. In the project both the Hebrew calendar and the Gregorian one are used. Still the Gregorian method is more evidential, using the large date's numbers of the month. Only holidays ("good days") are shown as a full number. What is the minimum number's part to expose according to be able to read it? What is the minimum one should do according to call it a day?

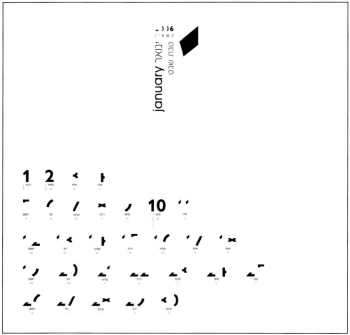

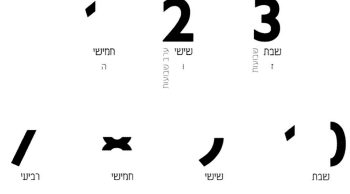

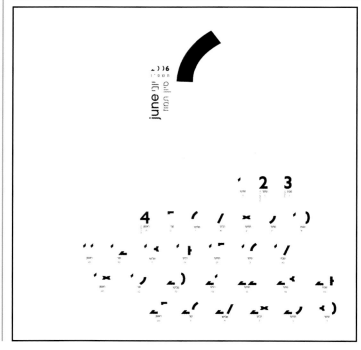

Design and copywriting: Mirit Wissotzky
Art direction: Manuel Dall'olio
Agency: AdmCom (Italy)

2009 Pershing Calendar

WORLD-MOVING IDEAS : There is neither a starting point, nor an ending point. Ideas have always existed, and they always will be. Each invention gives life to a future one. Great ideas are living among us, we just have to pause, look, touch and transform them into the next invention.

"World-moving ideas" is a celebration of the power of ideas.
The calendar presents 12 universally known objects and shows how many of the things that surround us today exist on account of important inventions in the past. Every object includes a description of the original idea that led to its invention, plus of course the month of the year 2009.

Produced in limited edition, the calendar has been sent to Pershing customers, prospects and opinion leaders.

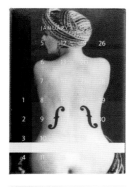

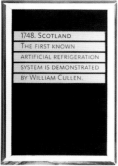

1748. SCOTLAND
THE FIRST KNOWN
ARTIFICIAL REFRIGERATION
SYSTEM IS DEMONSTRATED
BY WILLIAM CULLEN.

1908. SWITZERLAND
WHILE THE WAITER IS REPLACING THE
TABLECLOTH HE HAS SPILT WINE ON,
JACQUES E. BRANDENBERGER THOUGHT
OF INVENTING A CELLOPHANE FILM FOR
COATING CLOTH TO MAKE IT WATERPROOF.

1873. FRANCE
AROUND THE WORLD IN EIGHTY DAYS,
JULES VERNE'S CLASSIC ADVENTURE NOVEL,
IS PUBLISHED FOR THE FIRST TIME.

1855. USA
WHEN HIS WIFE BEGINS TO SUFFER
FROM CRIPPLING ARTHRITIS,
ANTONIO MEUCCI INSTALLS IN HIS
HOME THE FIRST EVER TELEPHONE
SYSTEM LINKING HER BEDROOM TO
HIS WORKSHOP.

1436. GERMANY
JOHANNES GUTENBERG
CHANGES THE WORLD OF
PRINTING BY INVENTING
THE PRINTING PRESS WITH
MOVEABLE WOODEN OR
METAL LETTERS.

5000 A.C. MESOPOTAMIA
SADLY THE NAME OF THE PERSON WHO FIRST
INVENTED THE WHEEL IS AN UNKNOWN.

PINO

1877. USA
THOMAS EDISON
DEMONSTRATES HIS
PHONOGRAPH, THE FIRST
MACHINE EVER TO RECORD
AND REPRODUCE SOUND.

1702. GERMANY
IN HIS OCULUS ARTIFICIALIS, JOHANN ZAHN ILLUSTRATES WHAT
SEEMS TO BE THE FIRST PAIR OF HAND-HELD BINOCULARS.

STAGIONE
2008
2009

Art Director: Milan Stojanov
Creative Director: Filip Unkovski
Managing Director: Ivan Unkovski
Account Director: Natasha Mitreva
Account Manager: Sladzana Medarova
BTL / Production Manager: Dushko Atanasovski
Photographer: Dejan Panovski

Rolling Pin Calendar 2010

THE BRIEF: To create a unique New Year promotional material and raise awareness for the World Wide Bakery brand, part of the Kadino Industry Group.

THE IDEA: Make a calendar on a rolling pin, thus share the love of baking with a memorable gift. When pressed upon dough the rolling pin leaves an impression of the year to come. It fits well with the company profile and makes a great gift for that can be used in the years to come.

THE RESULTS: The rolling pin calendar created a great buzz for the company. It generated vast international PR for World Wide Bakery. This in turn helped this company establish several key contacts with foreign distributors and markets for distributing of their products.

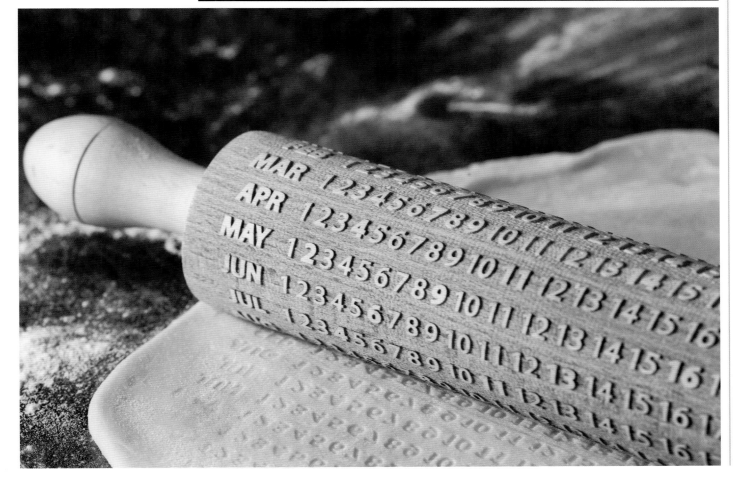

Experimental Calendar 2009

"I've been on a calendar but I have never been on time" (Marilyn Monroe). This experimental calendar gives you the overview on every following month and not only the current one. It works with holes and concentric rings. The smaller the circles, the less of the year is left. The color scheme matches the seasons.

Smyk is a Berlin-based design and illustration duo, consisting of Kai and Stephi.

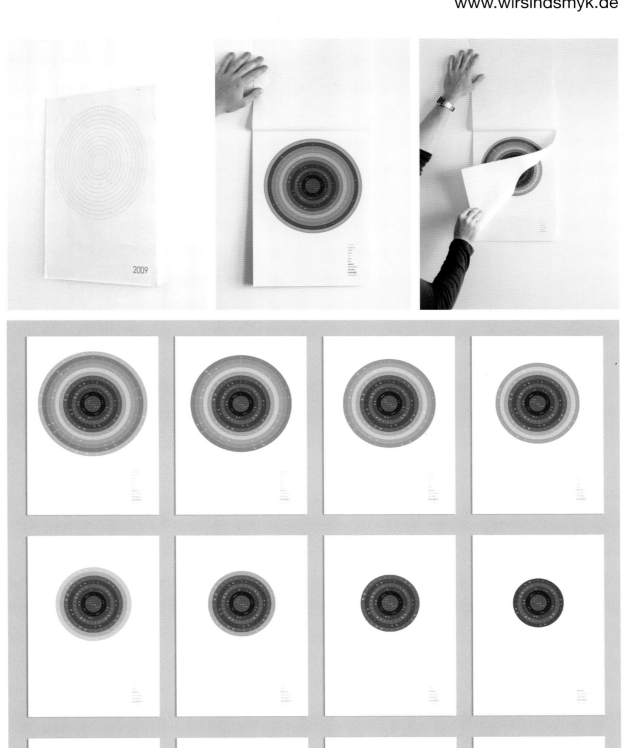

Igepa Calendar

Art Director / Designer: Tomislav Jurica Kacunic
Typography: Joel Nordström, Nikola Djurek

Ilgepa Calendar doesn't only show time but illustrates its flow, because by the passing of the months the visuals of the calendar also develop and move. With the change of each month the colors change as well. This calendar is unique because it's not printed and is made of skin paper. The numbers, the date markings, are laser-cut, which accentuates the exclusive skin paper structure, its special tactile and visual characteristics, so the paper itself is shown in its most pure, almost elementary form. Therefore, this is not just the Igepa Plana Papers calendar, but also an interesting catalogue, a live picture ephemeral as time itself.

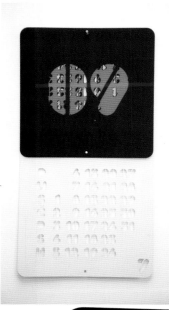
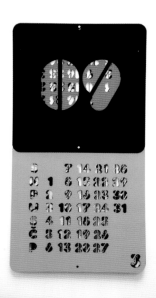

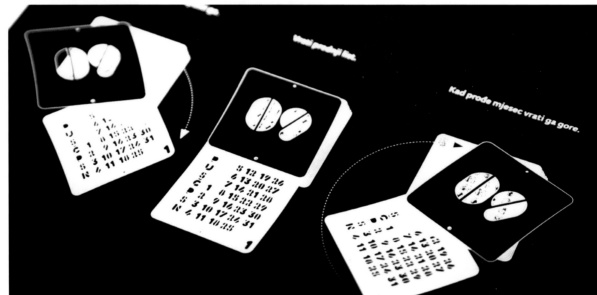

Kad prođe mjesec vrati ga gore.

oscar diaz

Ink Calendar

This calendar makes use of the timed pace of the ink spreading on the paper to indicate time. The ink is absorbed slowly, and the numbers in the calendar are "printed" daily. One a day, they are filled with ink until the end of the month. A self-updating calendar which enhances the perception of time passing not only signalling it. The materials used are paper and ink.

The ink colors are based on a spectrum which relates to a "color temperature scale", each month having a color related to our perception of the weather that month. The colors range from dark blue in December to three shades of green or oranges in spring, and red in the summer. The scale for measuring the "color temperature" that I have used is a standard called 'D65' and corresponds roughly to a midday sun in Western / Northern Europe.

Dimensions: 420 x 595 mm

2010 Calendar

A poster-calendar for 2010, with space to write important dates below each month. Printed using soy-based inks on a heavy recycled cover stock.

Dimensions: 16" x 16"

mash creative

www.mashcreative.co.uk

Limited Edition A1

The Calendar has been designed on an 8-column grid, the 'jumbled' text at the top reads "Thirty-one million, five hundred and fifty six thousand, nine hundred and twenty six seconds which is the number of seconds in a year. The title text at the top echoes that of an old analogue clock which is also shown in the bottom left corner of the calendar in the 2010 text. The poster was originally designed to be a self-promotional tool. The posters are printed with bi-color litho on 170gsm cyclus offset with a 60% cyan shiner to achieve an extra rich black. Each poster is hand numbered and signed by the designer.

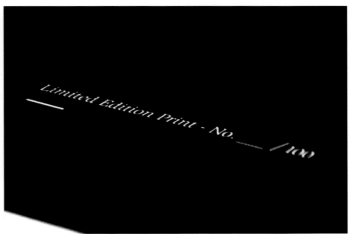

alex diaz

Experimental Typography Calendar

This calendar was a project for a Corcoran College of Art + Design Typography 2 class. The focus of this project was to redesign a calendar as the students saw fit. My concept was to deconstruct the calendar's typography and layout, and to challenge the viewer to use an experimental approach, that places more emphasis on the aesthetics.

Client: Corcoran College of Art + Design
Art Director & Designer: Alex Diaz

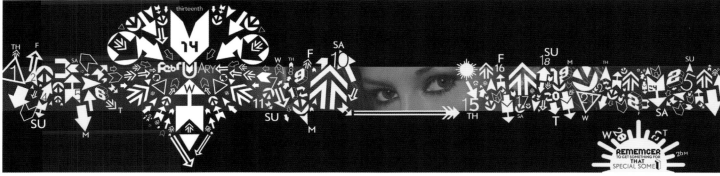

malota projects

www.malotaprojects.com

Malotaprojects 2009 Calendar

A limited edition wall calendar of which 300 copies are printed, signed and numbered by hand.
Mar Hernandez is an interdisciplinary artist and her work as an illustrator is one of her more
interesting skills, because her intense work and development in this field has defined her as an
important reference.

Dimensions: 15 x 29 cm

JANUARY / ENERO

MAY / MAYO

JULY / JULIO

AUGUST / AGOSTO

SEPTEMBER / SEPTIEMBRE

NOVEMBER / NOVIEMBRE

margarita bibilova

www.behance.net/Margarita

Desktop Calendar '09

The conception of the calendar consists of changing a usual, boring kind of a wall-calendar in a volumetrically interesting, functional and at the same time decorative desktop calendar. It can be used as a decorative element on the desk.

2010 Calendar

Our 2010 calendar features hand-drawn geometric illustrations unique to each month and is printed on 100lb acid-free card stock. It can function as a desk calendar, can be pinned to a bulletin board, framed, or even sent as a card.

PAWLING | print studio was created by sisters Trisha and Janet Snyder, who have backgrounds in architecture and graphic design respectively. Together they make handmade prints and patterns for the home. Based in Washington, DC, the studio focuses on environmentally responsible production as well as clean, understated design.

Dimensions: 4" x 6"

felix wong

www.portfolio.felixwong.net

Crossbird Calendar 2010

A self-initiated fund-raising calendar project. All proceeds went to World Relief (worldrelief.org), a respected international charity. The original screen-printed calendar sold in a limited edition of 80 sets. Printed entirely by hand on a Gocco printer on 12 colors of Paper Source cardstock (also hand cut). Because these are hand-printed, slight color and density variations exist between prints. This makes every calendar a unique and special piece of art. Accompanied by a mini bullfrog clip for easy hanging.

Felix's work is inspired by the simplicity of natural wonder, with a cuteness that's sure to put a smile on your face. He loves dreaming up stories and ideas behind each character and illustration he creates.

Dimensions: 3.5" x 8"

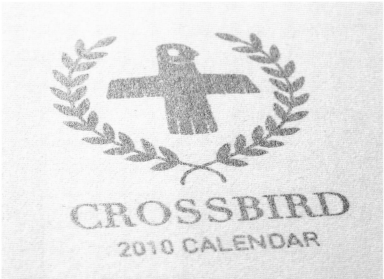

At the crossroads of European worlds Calendar 2008

Slovenia is so diverse that it cannot be described with just one or two features and we wonder how do others view it? Its diversity is reflected in all the spheres of man's endeavours – from material standing and social relationships, to spiritual creativity. It is reflected in the cultural-historical heritage as well as in contemporariness.

The contemporary creativity of Slovenia, partly presented by our calendar, can present a distinctive challenge to the entire European 'family', introducing the often still unknown values and riches to its variety and diversity. Discovering them brings spiritual enrichment and perception of values, which can co-shape the modern quality of man's existence and living.

Client: Kmecki glas, Ljubljana, Slovenia
Art direction and design: Edi Berk / KROG, Ljubljana
Text: Prof Dr Janez Bogataj
Photography: Dragan Arrigler

At the crossroads
of European worlds

2008

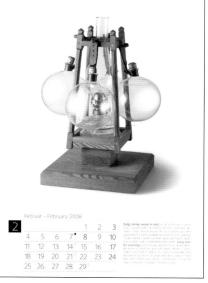

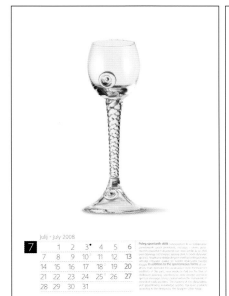

Julij · July 2008

7	1	2	3	4	5	6
	7	8	9	10	11	12	13
	14	15	16	17	18	19	20
	21	22	23	24	25	26	27
	28	29	30	31			

Poleg spontanih oblik naluzupomoči fit so številpomina prenesena iz steklo prevrednost. Vsa veča obliko skleraji stvorih ustvarjenih vrjetina lih. Istovrstno Naglj/naglj in-selo ijentinetrelo grudno uaci. Wickerwork is one of the oldest... **In addition to the spontaneous forms** of... according to the designs by the Nacglem Oslar Koga.

Avgust · August 2008

8					1	2	3
	4	5	6	7	8	9	10
	11	12	13	14	15	16	17
	18	19	20	21	22	23	24
	25	26	27	28	29	30	31

Tradicionalni lončarski izdelki... **In the modern day life.** Traditional pottery products have... container in mankind.

September · September 2008

9	1	2	3	4	5	6	7
	8	9	10	11	12	13	14
	15	16	17	18	19	20	21
	22	23	24	25	26	27	28
	29	30					

Spravilo pridelkov je bil vedno velik praznik... **Harvesting has always been a great holiday.** Because a holiday as well, this brocade ariform comments signifying... return.

April · April 2008

4		1	2	3	4	5	6
	7	8	9	10	11	12	13
	14	15	16	17	18	19	20
	21	22	23	24	25	26	27
	28	29	30				

Pletarstvo je ena najstarejših... **Wickerwork is one of the oldest** of... the synthesis of natural economy with natural materiality.

Maj · May 2008

5				1	2	3	4
	5	6	7	8	9	10	11
	12	13	14	15	16	17	18
	19	20	21	22	23	24	25
	26	27	28	29	30	31	

Največ skrivnosti je bilo od nekdaj... **The work of blacksmiths**... which combines a focus in the nowadays region.

Junij · June 2008

6							1
	2	3	4	5	6	7	8
	9	10	11	12	13	14	15
	16	17	18	19	20	21	22
	23/30	24	25	26	27	28	29

Oblinec, ki so jih pustčali mojstri in leseni... **Shavings, left over by joiners and carpenters**... to earn the wine forever.

Oktober · October 2008

10			1	2	3	4	5
	6	7	8	9	10	11	12
	13	14	15	16	17	18	19
	20	21	22	23	24	25	26
	27	28	29	30	31		

Žlica je še vedno temeljni pribor... **The spoon is still the basic tableware** for... for famous artists and the exclusive ones.

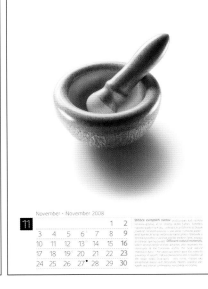

November · November 2008

11						1	2
	3	4	5	6	7	8	9
	10	11	12	13	14	15	16
	17	18	19	20	21	22	23
	24	25	26	27	28	29	30

Številče evropskih svetov... **Different natural materials**, which several people in their activities also represent the... support and improve professionally recycling the masters.

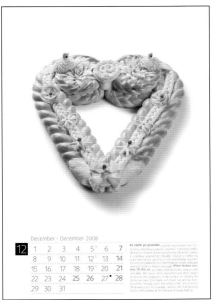

December · December 2008

12	1	2	3	4	5	6	7
	8	9	10	11	12	13	14
	15	16	17	18	19	20	21
	22	23	24	25	26	27	28
	29	30	31				

Ko zadnji po prazniku... **When festive season has**... the analysis for the increase reflecting self and stayed.

How to experience (feel) Slovenia? Calendar 2009

Seeing such a title and calendar theme makes us wonder at first: what does it actually mean?
To experience(feel) means living to see the material, social and spiritual discoveries upon making contact with Slovenia, a variegated, and in particular versatile, region and country at the meeting point between the European Alps, the Mediterranean and the Pannonian Plain.

It also means discovering the turbulent past and the broad spectrum of its cultural heritage, as well as the rich forms of contemporary creativity. It means breathtaking diversity of natural and urban areas, where the people of Slovenia live. The natural character of materials is the most basic authorial handwriting, a sign of recognition and identity, by which we not only co-shape our own image in the European and global family, but also enrich it with positive cultural and creative variety. Therefore, Slovenia is not only observed and visited, but truly experienced(felt)!

Client: Kmecki glas, Ljubljana, Slovenia
Art direction and design: Edi Berk / KROG, Ljubljana
Text: Prof Dr Janez Bogataj
Photography: Tomo Jesenicnik

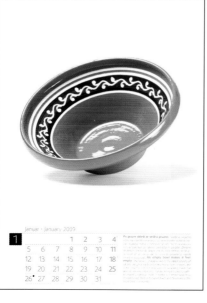

April · April 2009

4		1	2	3	4	5
	6	7	8	9	10	11	12
	13	14	15	16	17	18	19
	20	21	22	23	24	25	26
	27	28	29	30			

Maj · May 2009

5			1	2	3
	4	5	6	7	8	9	10
	11	12	13	14	15	16	17
	18	19	20	21	22	23	24
	25	26	27	28	29	30	31

Junij · June 2009

6	1	2	3	4	5	6	7
	8	9	10	11	12	13	14
	15	16	17	18	19	20	21
	22	23	24	25	26	27	28
	29	30					

Julij · July 2009

7		1	2	3	4	5
	6	7	8	9	10	11	12
	13	14	15	16	17	18	19
	20	21	22	23	24	25	26
	27	28	29	30	31		

Avgust · August 2009

8						1	2
	3	4	5	6	7	8	9
	10	11	12	13	14	15	16
	17	18	19	20	21	22	23
	24/31	25	26	27	28	29	30

September · September 2009

9		1	2	3	4	5	6
	7	8	9	10	11	12	13
	14	15	16	17	18	19	20
	21	22	23	24	25	26	27
	28	29	30				

Oktober · October 2009

10				1	2	3	4
	5	6	7	8	9	10	11
	12	13	14	15	16	17	18
	19	20	21	22	23	24	25
	26	27	28	29	30	31	

November · November 2009

11							1
	2	3	4	5	6	7	8
	9	10	11	12	13	14	15
	16	17	18	19	20	21	22
	23/30	24	25	26	27	28	29

December · December 2009

12		1	2	3	4	5	6
	7	8	9	10	11	12	13
	14	15	16	17	18	19	20
	21	22	23	24	25	26	27
	28	29	30	31			

Antalis Calendar 2010

Commissioned by Antalis (HK) Ltd to design a calendar for 2010, the designers set out to design a practical desk calendar to promote Antalis' fancy paper and 'Greening your business' concept, and came to innovate a new format of calendar which can be used as a monthly mini-schedule, but also as a desk calendar. All monthly schedules were printed with different effects to show the reaction between ink and paper, the information and diagrams show the positive concept and research of '2 sides of paper'. It educates the paper-buying public of the true facts so they can make informed choices and promotes responsible paper use.

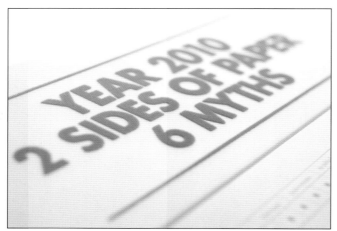

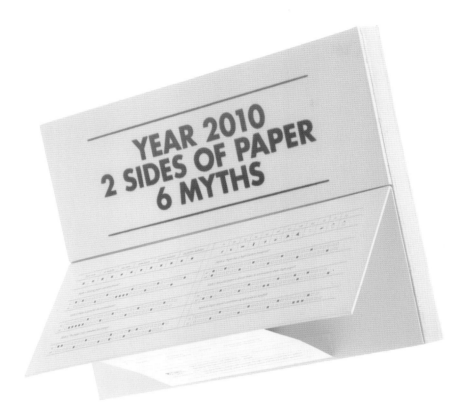

PI Calendar

The design and structure of this promotional calendar takes its cue from the concept of the mathematical PI symbol and its relation to eternity.

COLORATURA Calendar

This promotional calendar features the work of photographer Valerie Simmons and showcases the designer's season design campaign for the Canadian Opera Company.

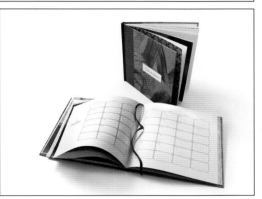

TOY STORY Calendar

Inspired by Christmas toy stories, this custom box set of calendar cards features an antique toy collection and the unique toy stories of each of our design team.

hansen belyea

www.hansenbelyea.com

2005 Year of the Rooster Calendar

Inspired by the coming Year of the Rooster, designer Ben Reynolds created the chicken in the Mao jacket by making a collage with color laser copies. The rest of the calendar art was made with real 3-D objects: gold spray-painted picture frames, fans and leaves; toy Chinese lanterns cut in half; red tissue paper; and Chinese newspapers. The tabletop composition was photographed in a commercial studio to ensure that the lighting on the metallic objects was just right. Working with the digital image, the type was added for the calendar title, months and dates. The one-sided calendar folded flat as one set of side panels was slightly narrower than the other. The calendar slipped into a custom envelope with an end flap for mailing.

Client: Hansen Belyea
Strategic Director: Patricia Belyea
Design Director: Ron Lars Hansen
Designer: Ben Reynolds
Illustrator: Ben Reynolds

Client: Hansen Belyea
Strategic Director: Patricia Belyea
Design Director: Ron Lars Hansen
Designer: Ben Reynolds
Illustrator: Ron Lars Hansen, nicholas Johnson

2006 Cultivate Calendar

Playing with the similarities between branding and farming, Hansen Belyea's 2006 promotional calendar focused on the theme "Cultivate." Sow Now, Irrigate Often, and Harvest the Mother Lode are headlines on illustrated divider panels. Different styles of illustrations were created to add texture to the Z-fold calendar. A custom square envelop, printed on a lighter weight paper, was used to mail the calendar.

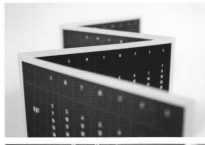

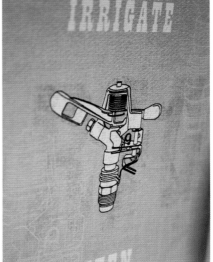

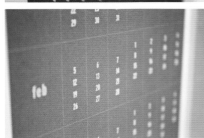

hansen belyea

www.hansenbelyea.com

2007 tower Calendar

Experimenting with paper structures, the four-sided paper tower with a half-height sleeve was chosen as the favorite. The structure was especially appealing as the sleeve dropped down to reveal additional graphics when the calendar was flipped over. Working with Sculpey clay, four characters were created—that illustrated different aspects of our studio's methodology - Strategy, Creativity, Passion, Playfulness. Printed on a pearlescent paper, the calendar and mailing envelope glow.

Client: Hansen Belyea
Strategic Director: Patricia Belyea
Design Director: Ron Lars Hansen
Designer: Ron Lars Hansen
Illustrator/Lettering Artist: Nicholas Johnson
Structural Designer: Kara Mealy

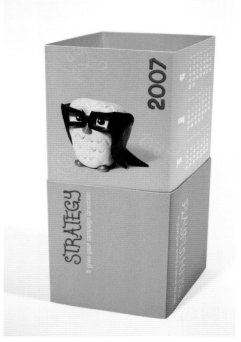

Client: Hansen Belyea
Strategic Director: Patricia Belyea
Design Director: Ron Lars Hansen
Designer: Ron Lars Hansen
Copywriter: Aaron Clifford
Illustrator: Ron Lars Hansen
Structural Designer: Nicholas Johnson

2009 impeller Calendar

The Impeller Calendar delivers two messages to clients. The first is a global theme as each "paddle" of the impeller features the national holiday of a distant country. The second is technical expertise. The engineering of the desktop calendar required a series of prototypes and laser die-cutting to get the pieces to lock together perfectly. The Impeller package consisted of four parts—the interlocking calendar parts, instructions with little diagrams, a custom die-cut carrier, and a sealing label.

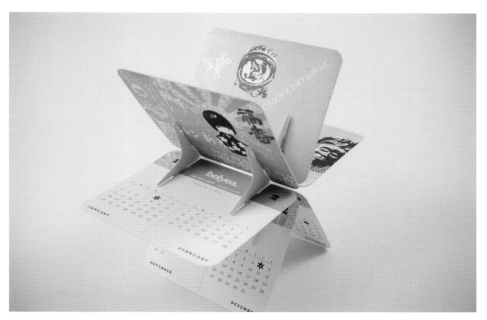

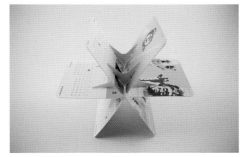

Set a date with LEGO in 2010

Love LEGO® bricks and minifigures? Now's your chance to enjoy them 365 day of the year! LEGO UK launched its first ever charity calendar. It featured a variety of LEGO mini figures, often pictured coming up against everyday objects, in twelve seasonal scenes. A fun way to start your day while benefiting a great cause, as LEGO UK donated all profits from the sale of this calendar to the National Autistic Society, the UK's leading charity for people with autism and their families.

Art Director / Designer / Photographer: Ben Watts

good morning inc

Rocking Chair Calendar

Rocking chair is a freestanding desktop calendar. Follow the guide to assemble rocking chair that rocks back and forth just like a real one.

Module Calendar

Fit the individual pieces together like a puzzle to make cube-shaped modules, then join the three modules to complete a calendar in a tower form.

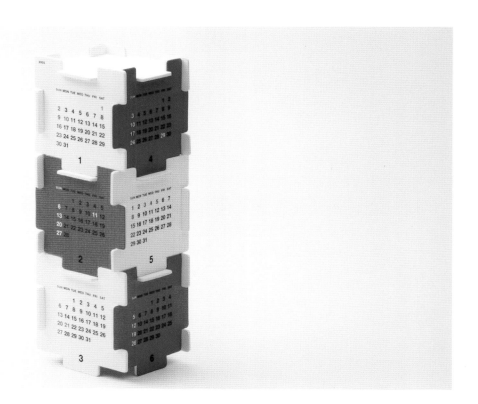

Safari Calendar

Safari is a paper animal calendar. Each of the six sheets shows two months - press out the parts and assemble to complete.

Waterwheel Calendar

Waterwheel is a three dimensional calendar made from six paddles in the shape of a waterwheel. Rotate a stand alone calendar each month.

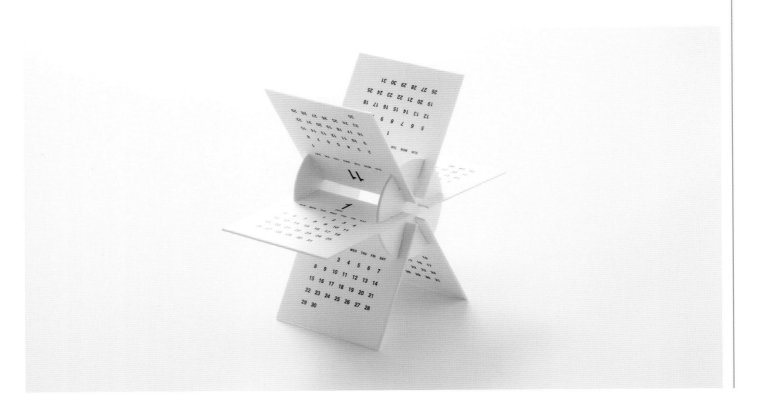

good morning inc
www.goodmorning.co.jp

Zoo Calendar

Zoo is a paper craft kit for making a one-year calendar consisting of six animals. No glue or scissors needed to build the calendar.

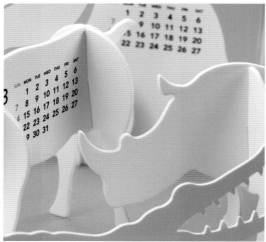

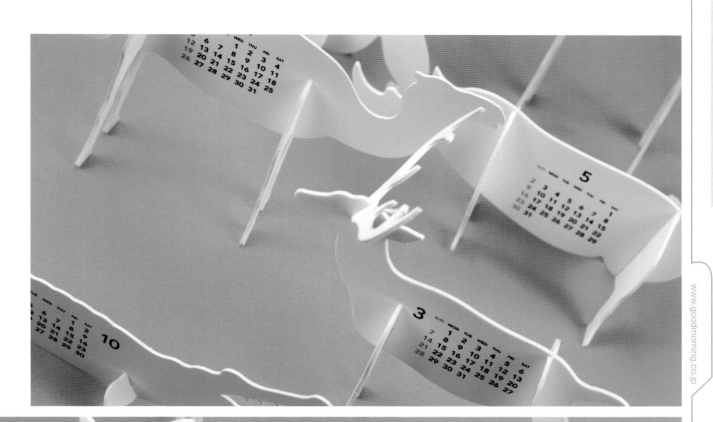

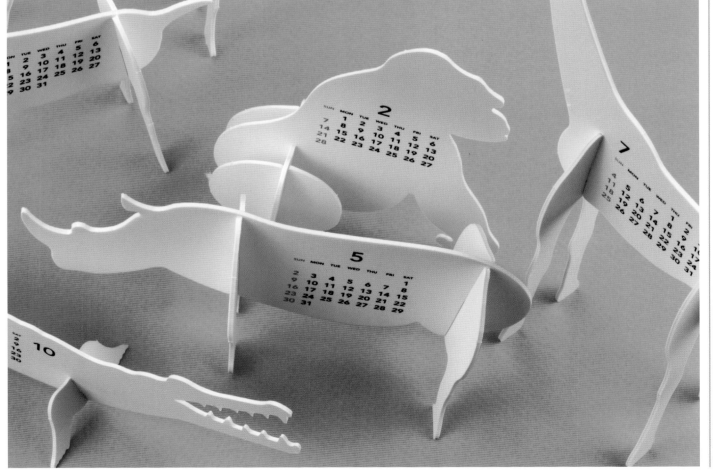

www.mikimono.es

Self edited 2010 Calendar

When Mónica León looked back on her work from year 2009 her wish to print it on paper suddenly grew strong, so she picked out her favourite illustrations to make her own unique calendar, which was printed in a 50-copy-limited edition and put together by hand.

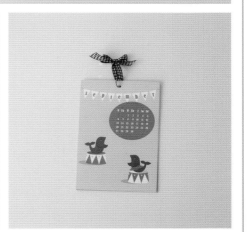

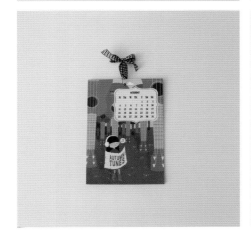

www.typodarium.de

Typodarium 2010

A source of daily typographic inspiration, Typodarium calendar is the first tear-off calendar with 365 different fonts by 180 foundries and designers; bread and butter types, character sets, old masters and wild youths from all over the world. A total of 370 pages - printed on both sides. On the front page are traditional and functional usages of day, date and month while on the back you´ll find background information and details about the designers and sources – and even a marriage proposal! It also has the bank holidays of 30 countries and a box to collect the sheets.

Dimensions: 8.5 x 12 cm

Editors: Lars Harmsen
(www.magmabranddesign.de),
Raban Ruddigkeit
(www.ruddigkeit.de)
Art Director / Project Management: Boris Kahl

two brunettes

www.twobrunettesshop.com

Two Brunettes Calendar

The calendar by Carolynn Giordano was a mixed media piece. Screen printed on white canvas with soy based inks. The calendar is hung with silver grommets and sea foam green grosgrain ribbon.

Two Brunettes is a stationery and design studio based in central NY. Whatever the project is, big or small, it can be created. We specialize in wedding and party invitations of all kinds, branding packages large and small, logos, web design, and custom blog designs.

Client: RJ Paper, Kin Yiap Press

Twenty O'Eight Planner

From cover to cover, every space is utilised: 365 days at a glance on the cover; Holidays fill the spine; The ends made up of monthly and conversion charts. Inside, there's monthly, weekly and daily calendars along with gridded, dotted and blank pages. A custom typeface – a modification of Avant Garde with each letter receiving different layers depending on its place in the alphabet – liberally applied to every inch (including the page edges). Materials and techniques involved: Edge-printing, elastic band, kiss-cut adhesive and three other paper stock.

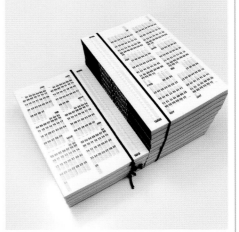

LHN 2009 Calendar

Client: LHN Group
Photography: Pinckers Pte Ltd

The brief was to create two calendars: an english and a chinese version. The solution combines both into one, and the result is a dual-purpose desktop and wall calendar with a double cover. The chinese version on one side is designed to replicate the traditional chinese calendar. The english side looks and feels the opposite. The colored tabs (which also represent the secondary graphics of LHN Group's brand) serve as easy reference, and form a layered composition of both languages. Materials and techniques involved: Duplex and die cut.

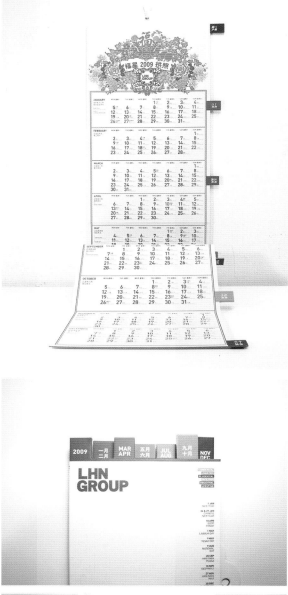

Client: RJ Paper, A&D Printhub

Twenty Ten Planner

A follow-up on the planner designed in Twenty O'Eight for RJ Paper. Materials & techniques involved: Rainbow foil-stamping, edge-printing and five different paper stock.

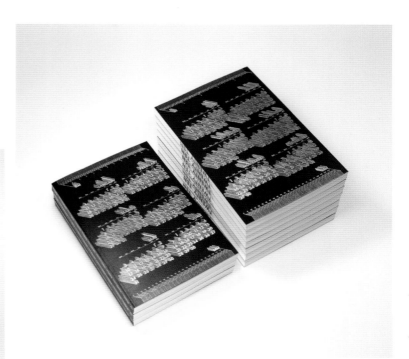

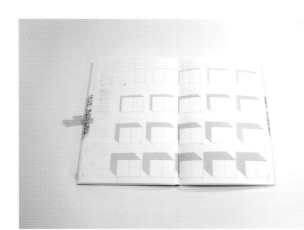

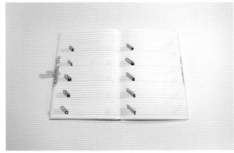

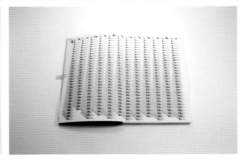

yurko gutsulyak

www.gstudio.com.ua

Walking Calendar (2008)

Client: Huggies (Kimberly-Clark Ukraine)

A calendar to represent HUGGIES brand philosophy and values: joy, pleasure, and freedom of discovery of the wonderful world. HUGGIES allows a baby to walk easily through the life and ignore the "small problems" that might happen. We created an idea of two "baby's feet" that move along the page imitating the baby's steps and marking the current day. Every page shows simple things from which a baby starts to learn the world. That's how we expressed the freedom of motion and the process of baby's development. Every new day is a step forward.

Client: VS Energy International Ukraine

Colour Calendar (2008)

The text on the cover: "The world around us is full of colors and each color in the world emits the energy inherent only to it. We see BUSINESS AS ART of searching for own color combinations and creating with their help of own world". While creating the calendar it was essential to concentrate on the energy that is implied in the name and logo of the company and it was necessary to use the existing slogan, "Business as an Art". We suggested the idea of "Colour calendar", each page of which is dedicated to a particular color and its energy. This idea allows us to represent and explain the symbiosis of Energy, Business and Art. It should be noted that the idea is not a new one and improvisations on it can be found in portfolios of numerous design studios. That is why it was important for us to find a brand new way to present this idea, a way that would make this calendar unique and special. As one turns the pages, bright colorful patterns emerge: these were created on the basis of traditional patterns of Ukrainian atrs and crafts.

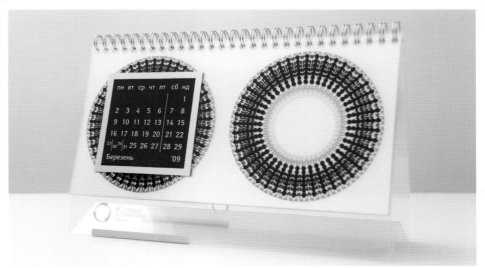

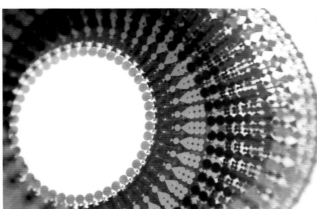

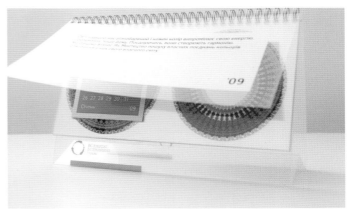

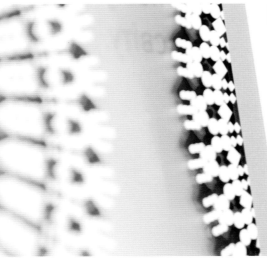

yurko gutsulyak

The idea was to create a calendar so unique that the process of its presentation would become an outstanding event. Alongside this, it was important to expose the idea of "energy", as it is predetermined by the name and logo of the company. Each page is a month and looks like a comb made of matches that correspond to the days. The matches are real and the construction of the calendar is absolutely safe.

Client: VS Energy International Ukraine

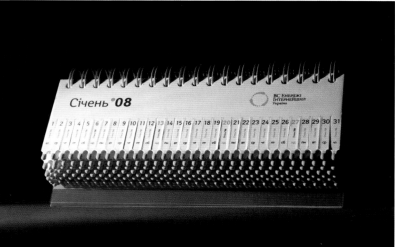

Client: Dalnoboy

Tyre Fitting Calendar (2009)

Dalnoboy (Long-distance trucker) is the widest truck tyre service network in the CIS countries. The principal objective of the company is to increase the tyre run. So Dalnoboy seeks to make the tyres "everlasting". This concept inspired us to create an "everlasting" Tyre Fitting Calendar. An "asphalted" box contains an envelope with component parts, and on the envelope there is a detailed printed guidance on calendar assembly, application, repair and warranty service. The calendar is absolutely interactive, though little effort is required to use it. Every day it is necessary to move only one wheel-day. And set a mark in front of the appropriate month name once in a month. The kit also has a spare wheel to replace a "day" should it be lost. The guidance provides a phone number of the Dalnoboy's customer service. Beside the usual servives, one can get advice on Tyre Calendar assembly and usage, and also order spare parts.

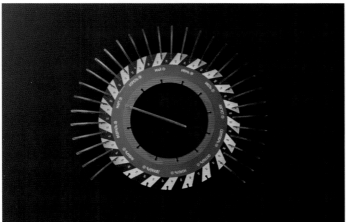
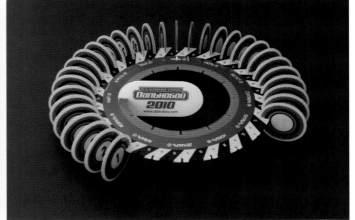
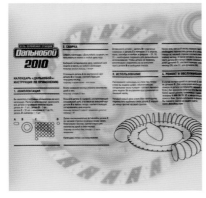

www.nanocadesign.com

The beautiful "Kasane no irome," color arrangement, was formed by aesthetic consciousness of aristocrats in the Heian period. There are two widely held interpretations of kasane no irome. One refers to a color that was made by combining both sides of a lined kimono and the other refers to a color arrangement that was formed when many kimonos were layered. Kasane no irome is a sophisticated color culture that takes four seasons in Japan into consideration. In this calendar, kasane no irome, expressed by aristocrats in the old days with kimonos, is modernized. Enjoy the colors that reflect the feeling of each month and the culture of aristocrats in the Heian period such as names of Japanese traditional colors in your room.
Product recommended as a gift for New Year or year's end.

Designer: Sumiko Endo

Family Crest Calendar 2010

It was about 800 years ago when family crests first appeared in Japan. First, the aristocratic and samurai classes used them and in early modern ages they spread into common usage. Now, there are about 20,000 family crests recorded in books. I selected pretty and humorous animal crests from among the enormous material and made an auspicious calendar with them. The calendar is composed of existing completed crests, texts describing reasons why they are auspicious, and Japanese traditional colors. Old culture and modern design are combined in the family crest calendar. Please enjoy the pretty family crests that are placed in each month of the calendar. It is recommended to use this calendar as a gift for New Year or year's end.

The supplied tape is made of environment-friendly paper. It is possible to contribute to a small percentage of CO_2 emission reduction by switching from a cellophane tape to a paper tape. This is very small efforts but I would like to spread this activity as a designer and seller of paper products. It is recommended to reuse the paper box as a small toolbox after the calendar is finished. "Noshi" (a long thin strip of paper attached to a gift) is attached to the box of the product. Due to the Noshi, you do not need to gift-wrap the product, when you use it for a gift. This calendar was made by incorporating Japanese culture and in consideration of CO_2 emission reduction, the modern environmental problem.

paweł piłat

www.jaktokto.com

Multifaith Calendar 2010

This multi-faith calendar includes the religions Bahaism, Buddhism, Christianity, Hinduism, Mormonism, Islam, Jainism, Judaism, Paganism, Rastafarianism, Sikhism, Shintoism, Zoroastrianism.

Dimensions: 100 x 70 cm

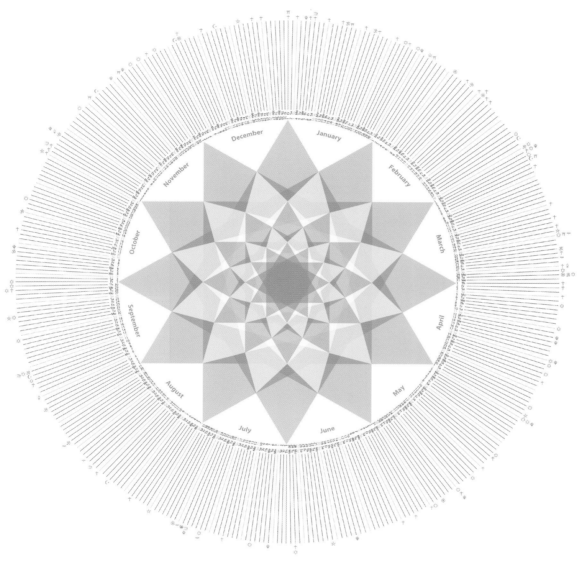

Multifaith calendar for 2010

www.magnoliamoonlight.com

Designer: Christina Flowers

Shout Calendar

The Magnolia Moonlight Shout calendar embraces luscious colors that reflect each season. Playful and fun to make you smile when adding important dates or little reminders to your agenda. The little bird is a constant companion, guiding you through the year month by month. It is a twelve month wall calendar printed double sided on 100% recycled paper with vegetable based inks. Dimensions: 9" x 11.5"

www.magnoliamoonlight.com

magnolia moonlight

Calendar of Important Dates

For All The Days That Mean Something to YOU! Never forget a birthday, anniversary or any other important date again with this twelve month calendar that never goes out of date! This eco-friendly calendar is printed on 100% recycled paper using soy inks.

Dimensions: 4" x 11.5"

Talk Calendar, Feather Calendar, Lemon Tree Calendar, Orange Vines Calendar

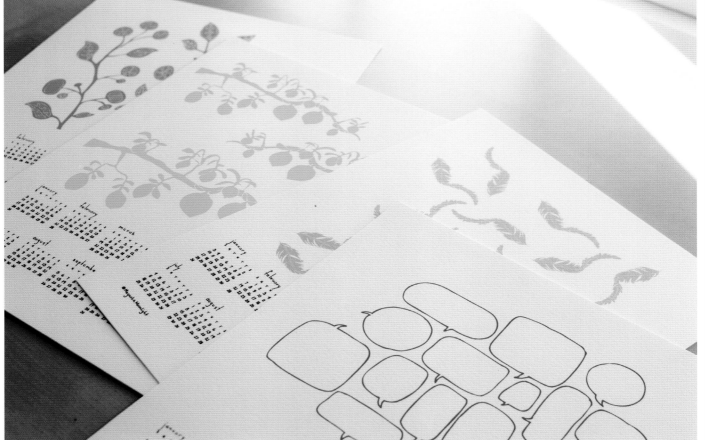

magnolia moonlight

www.magnoliamoonlight.com

Humming Bird

The Magnolia Moonlight 2010 calendar prints showcase a design focus on color, beauty, inspiration and pattern. Each calendar has the whole year written in a hand-illustrated font and is printed on beautiful, textured, archival paper and comes with a signature of the designer.

Dimensions: 8x10

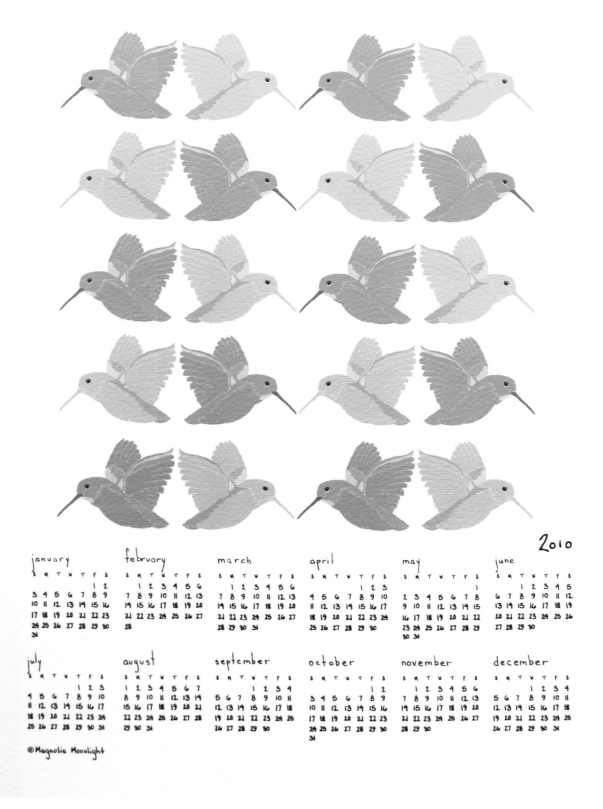

© Magnolia Moonlight

The Oh So Smitten 2010 calendar prints showcase a design focus on color, inspiration and pattern with a bit of playful fun . Each calendar has the whole year written in a hand-illustrated font and is printed on beautiful, textured, archival paper. and comes with a signature of the designer

Dimensions: 8x10

Smil-ring Calendar

Happy days provided by "Smil-ring" This 6-piece reversible calendar covers 12 months. Simply structured, just hooking the tag legs into the ring creates various motifs to suit to you. Accessory hat included. Use as an eye-catcher for the current month. A 6 page calendar + 1 accessory cap made of YUPO® paper

Dimensions: (C) 94 mm x 99 mm (P) 364 mm x 215 mm

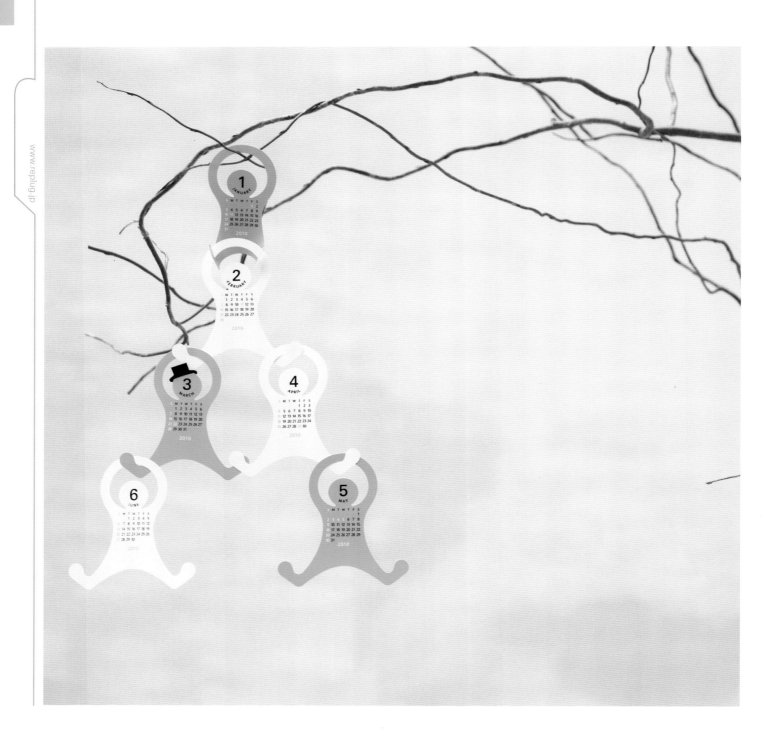

Pieces Calendar

Poster style calendar changes every day. Design changes every day by cutting off the pieces. Collection of your special day pieces is an alternative. The base sheet becomes a decorative ornament after all the pieces are removed. Two page with perforated tear off lines between days per page.

Dimensions: 515 mm x 728 mm

TYPOLIC Calendar

Memory, foresight, and rhythm - It's an endless time map. A permanent calendar featuring the beauty of typefaces - Avenir and Jenson were used. You can use this sophisticated aluminum / acrylic art calendar forever.

Dimensions: 325mm x 728mm x 55mm, 1300g/1450g

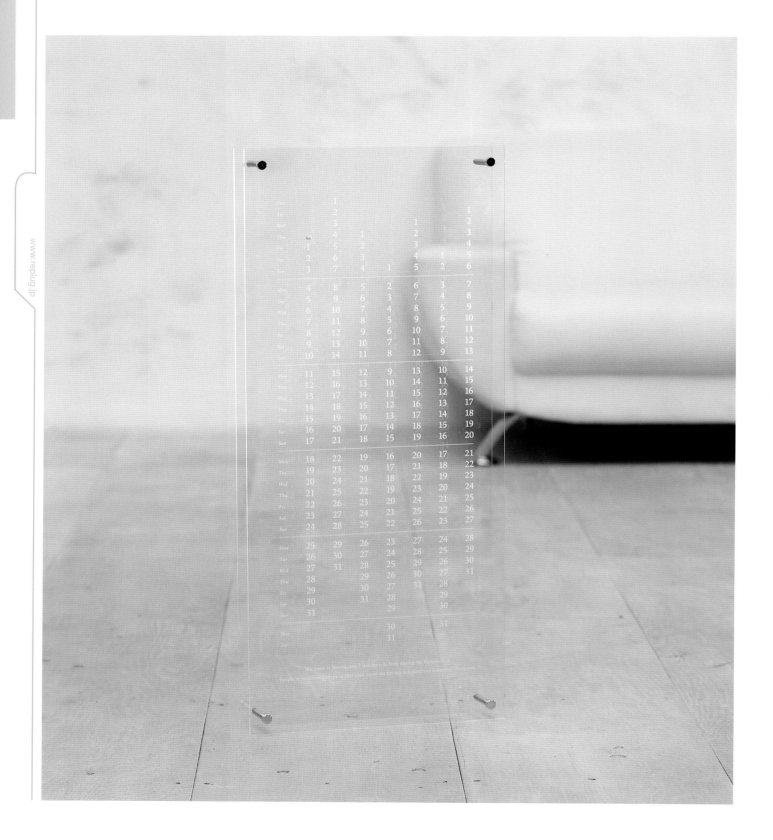

Earth in the room Calendar

Earth in the room. Earth in a frame. Artwork in the room. Favorite soothing calendar. Trees and animals are painted in the frame. Luminous painted stars shine in the dark night. Enjoy peaceful moments in your room. Consists of 1 luminous painted frame and 6 calendar pages.

Dimensions: 255mm x 364mm

sal azad

Happy Tiger Year - Papertoy Calendar

Dimensions: 14 cm x 6 cm x 11 cm (L x W x H)

Disco 2010 - Robo Papertoy Calendar

Dimensions: 7.5 cm x 7 cm x 16 cm (L x W x H)

Balloon AA Calendar

Live for today. Plan for tomorrow. Party tonight! Commissioned by Balloon AA (Balloon AA company).

Creative Director: Danuthas Thamaraksa
Copywriters: Nanthawat Mankong, Gop Sihsobhon, Danuthas Thamaraksa
Art Directors: Danuthas Thamaraksa, Lexaky Nawin
Photographer: Dan T.
Retoucher: Tora Studio

" Live For Today...Plan For Tomorrow...Party Tonight..!!!"
Anand Singh

Brief

Balloon AA are professional activity in every events. We wanted to communicate our product benefits to premium clients, the idea will make our clients to remind every their activities all the year.

Idea

We came up with Balloon AA calendar box set that contains 12 balloons as a premium gift. As our calendar - scheduled life is deteriorating our well - being, let the party bring our joy back to life again. Especially our clients turn a stressful office into a 365 - day of party.

BalloonAA calendar will perfectly help them remember schedules and activities, it also lightens up the party mood every time the clients look at Balloon AA blow up.

Calendar Tape

Multi-functional sticky tape that works as a calendar, diary, organiser & planner. As well as being pretty useful packaging tape! Easily create each month in any day and date combination, by using the two seperate rolls and sticking them next to each other.

superkonductor

www.superkonductor.com

2008 Time Out Chicago Magazine Calendar

Time-Out Chicago Magazine asked SuperKonductor to create this exclusive limited-edition calendar for their Holiday Gift Guide. 19x19 silkscreened calendar printed on French 100# Sand paper

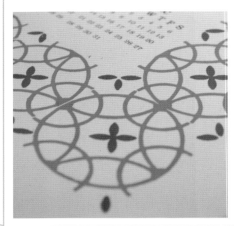

2009 Lotsa Dots Calendar

Featured in Time-Out Chicago Magazine, as well as popular blogs such as FFFFound!, Apartment Therapy Chicago, the Chicago Reader, and OMG Posters! among others. 19x25 silkscreened calendar printed on French 100# Sweet Tooth paper

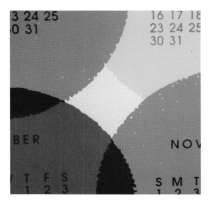

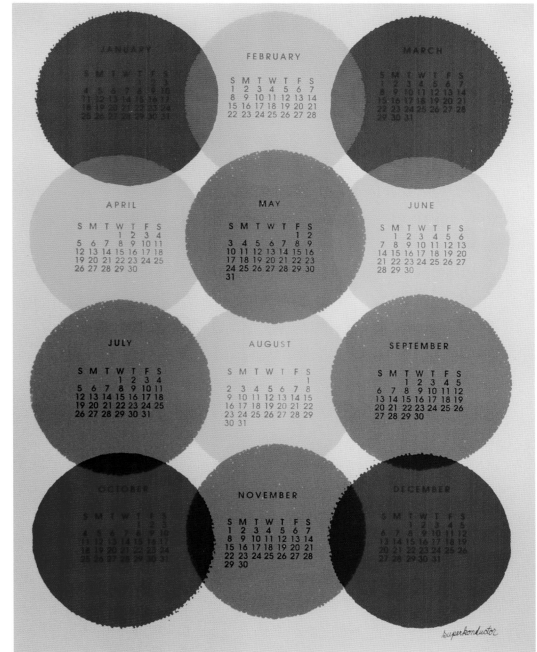

I'm not a calendar

We have collaborated with digital artist Simon Page to produce a desk calendar that is original, recyclable, expresses our unique approach to design, and above all useful long-term. The calendar features digital illustrations of geometric cubes, where pages are folded in such a way that they are reusable as posters or gift-wrap.

www.eiga.de

Think Green Calendar

The calendar shows contemporary "Eco typography" and special "green works" from different creative disciplines. Sustainability, recycling and renewable energy are among the central ideas of our time. In their work, designers see the growing challenge of how to safeguard our environment from very different points of view.

In this free design project, we created a visual environmental inventory. More than 100 designers from different creative disciplines are published and 53 designers get a special platform as a weekly motif. In their own way, each of the item is concerned with how we can manage our planet responsibly. We have created an individual typographic style for each calendar week in the context of raw materials, energy and the environment. This project is realized in cooperation with partners involved in the paper, print and processing sectors.

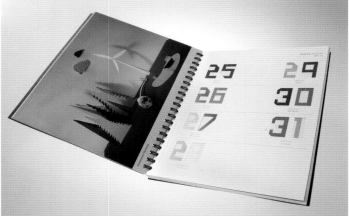

www.demianconrad.com

Gregory Calendar

Client: Calendar-Game

Gregory Calendar is a playful and funny calendar which you can communicate with, thanks to a super-white chubby pencil. At the start of each month, a black page appears which contains numbered small white circles in apparently untidy way. Everyday you must draw a line dot to dot following the number order. A magic character appears in this way. Thus at the end of each month, one of the twelve of Gregory's friends takes shape through the line more over, you can personify and colour your calendar with your pencils at home. The calendar can be personalized with reminders (in order to indicate important dates or meetings / rendezvous) and ornamental drawings (small flowers, mountains..) In this calendar, the year is not defined, therefore you can start it whenever you want. You can colour the small dots indicating the days so that week-ends, bank holidays, birthdays or school holidays are clear.

www.demianconrad.com

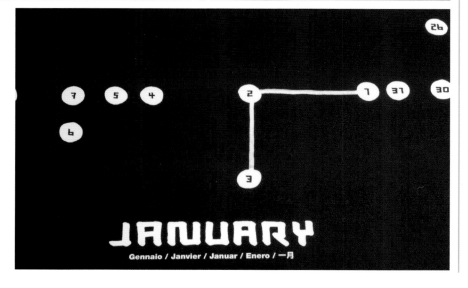

demian conrad design

www.demianconrad.com

Client: Calendar-Game

The ecological game Gaia is a calendar and a game with a learning purpose, on the theme of ecology. During 365 days, Gaia and their friends will awake the small green flame inside you and will help you in ta king good habits in favor of the environment.

INTERACTIVE: Gaia invites you to modify your daily behavior. Every month, you'll have four good actions to carry out in taking care of our planet; from waste disposal and recycling to water management, not forgetting saving energy. INFORMATIVE: Gaia shows you week by week the important appointment of ecology and supplies you with key information concerning the impact of the human activity on the environment. LUDIC: Gaia is first of all a game with the purpose of having a good time with the family or with friends, and appointing the person who by the end of the year will have the best eco-balance.

www.demianconrad.com

studio on fire
pg
099
www.studioonfire.com

2008 Illustrations by: Studio On Fire,
Colorblok, Brian Gunderson,
Rinzen, Justin Blyth, Harmen Liemburg

2008 Calendar

Late in 1999, Studio On Fire began letterpress printing in a cold Minnesota basement. Our first press occupied a spot between the boiler and the litter box. And oh how the studio has grown - now seven presses and seven people strong with a proper studio space we celebrate ten years as a bustling design and print studio.

2009 Calendar

2009 Illustrations by: Studio On Fire,
Adam Garcia, Brian Gunderson,
Rinzen, Justin Blyth, Clarimus

2010 Illustrations by: Studio On Fire,
Cecilie Ellefsen, Brian Gunderson,
The Little Friends of Printmakng,
ghostpatrol, Rilla Alexander (Rinzen)

2010 Calendar

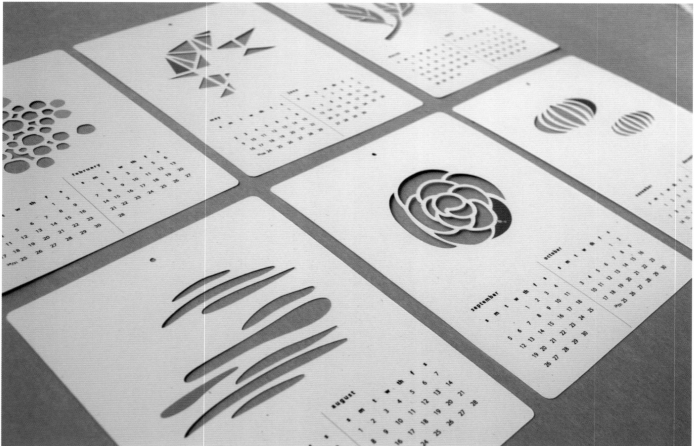

Remember Every Typeface

The call to resolutely remember and pay attention to details is whimsically presented in bloom studio's 2009 calendar. With a different typeface to depict each month, the individual characteristics of the typefaces bring the otherwise mundane months to life. This is a refreshing take on getting one to pay attention to being meticulous in the pursuit of perfection. By presenting the months in a broadsheet, the versatility goes beyond a mere calendar, inviting one to use it in a variety of ways - prettying up a dull package is one excellent example.

Dimensions: A1 size

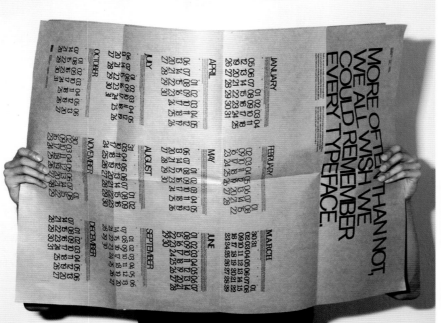

MORE OFTEN THAN NOT,
WE ALL WISH WE
COULD REMEMBER
EVERY TYPEFACE.

don't be shy

www.dontbeshy.com.ar

2010 Calendar

We thought of a piece in which several art styles can coexist and mark the difference for each month. We invited 13 artist/illustrators/designers that enjoy to taking part in self-managed group projects to participate. Each part involved the silkscreening process, choosing colors and feeling free to design their month designated randomly. Each month was printed in 2 colors. The calendar has an edition of 200 copies, the size is 17 x 20 cm (closed).

January: JoseGonzalez
February: Pedro Perelman / Bleep
March: Mariano Ferro
April: Nico Whelan
May: Valeria Boquete
June: Federico Pazos
July: Andre Calvente
August: Gabriela Sternberg
September: TEC
October: Valeria Montero
November: Ana Gilligan
December: Tester
January 2011: Sebastian Lahera

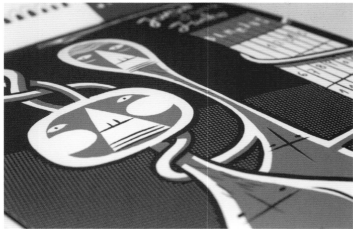

dark design group

www.darkdesign.ru

Large Lakes of Russia

Calendar 'Rosvodresursy - The largest lakes and water basins of Russia - is unique. Beauty and utility have merged together. Each page of the calendar is full of curious information and watercolour droplets formed a symbol of 2010 - a wonderful tiger.

Transparent Calendar

For ourselves, we've created a calendar that fades as each new page flips through the year.

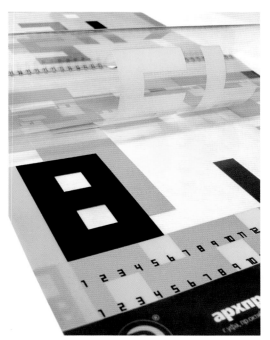

nothing design group

www.designnothing.com

Calendar with Vase

Give your home a new look by adding a decorative element to the calendar that always hangs on your wall. Just by placing a single flower in your calendar, you will feel your home get brighter. When you receive a flower as a gift and don't know where to put it, or when you want to appreciate the different flowers that come with different seasons, the Calendar with Flowerpot is the perfect choice. (An image in a calendar becomes a real object. A calendar becomes another kind of flowerpot. Is it a flowerpot? Or, is it a calendar?)

Closed: W135 x L430 x T15 mm
Opened: W135 x L860 x T15 mm

Material: Paper & E.V.A foam & glass

Designer: Koo Jin-woog
(director of NOTHING design group)

2010 Pocket Size Calendar

Designer: Kaoru

Small card size 2010 calender with each month illustrated with the month's flower motif. Numbers are UV printed on top.

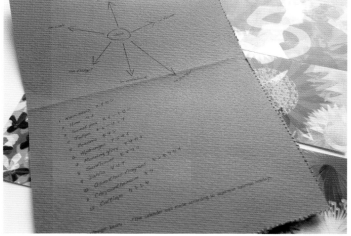

www.saar-ontwerp.nl

BNO Calendar

A calendar for the Association of Dutch Designers.

A Colouful Year

An A6 concertina-folded calendar that gives the viewer a real sense of the changing months and seasons through the use of colour. Each month is defined by a keyword and color that sums up the weather during those 4 weeks. The calender was designed as a self-promotional piece that design studios would receive and the idea was that people would keep it throughout the year.

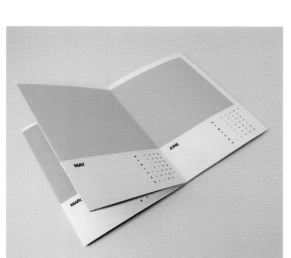

Cai Guo-Qiang Matches Calendar (2010)

Collaborating with international artist Cai Guo-Qiang, Eslite Corporation has adapted ideas from Cai's Crocodile and Sun to create the Matches Calendar/ Two Thousand and Ten as a gift for Eslite members. Cai Guo-Qiang is known as one of the leading contemporary artists of today. With his signature use of gunpowder, he celebrates the human spirit and its exchange with the larger universe around it by showing "the traces of fire and process of explosion in time and space." Eslite Corporation has taken the rich tradition of fireworks in Chinese culture and Chinese New Year to create a work that represent happiness, anticipation and a fleeting yet joyful moment. For the Calendar, Eslite Corporation used the shape of fireworks to present Eastern culture, Chinese red willow paper to show the uniqueness of the artist's hand, and the symbolic "red" and "fire" to illustrate Cai's enthusiasm for art. It consists of 365 matches to coincide with the 365 days of the year, with every single match igniting one's passion for each day.

Produced in: Taiwan
Artwork Authorized: Cai Studio
Designed: Verso

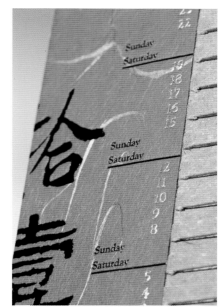

yanghee kang

www.yhkang.com

Your Univers for 2009

'Your Univers for 2009' is a promotional calendar for the Univers typeface. By breaking the shape & form of the original typeface and creating three-dimensional depth through the folded paper, the basic typeface becomes an unexpectedly interesting composition. Paper becomes a means for pulling out the unique aesthetics of the distorted typeface. This approach shows the essential aesthetics of the typeface without any other graphic elements.

Supervising professor: Prof. Eunsun Lee
University: Pratt Institute, New York

www.graphitica.com

Jagda Calendar Salone 2011

The calendar for each month generally reuses parts of the previous months' date indications. Variously shaped cutouts in each of the sheets reveal parts of the previous months' dates, which, together with the dates on the topmost sheet, make up the calendar for the current month. None of the single sheets work alone, but only when combined do they show the calendar for the current month in a variety of designs.

Based on the philosophy of "knowing new things by studying the old", this style was implemented with the aim to suggest to those who look at the calendar that "yesterday is feeding today and tomorrow." The basic composition adopts the style of a perpetual calendar. All months can be displayed by sliding the sheets.
The calendar sheets are connected through cutouts in each plate that reveal parts of each layer underneath.

GRAPHITICA inc is founded by Kazunori Gamo in 2008.

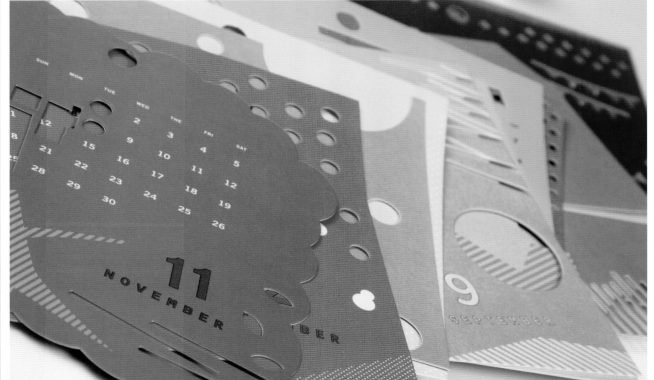

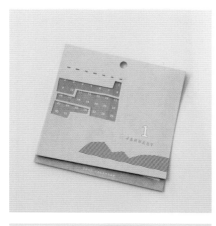
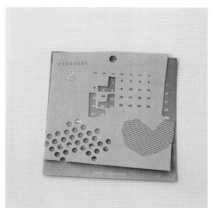

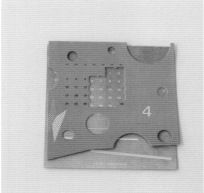
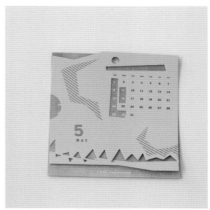

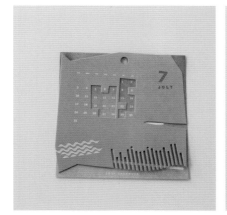
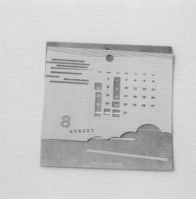
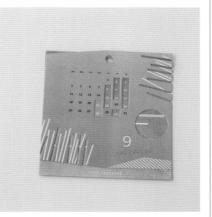
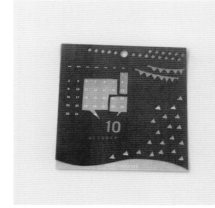

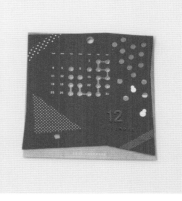

www.valerydesignwrks.ca

2009 Valerydesignwrks Illustrative Calendar

Designer: Valéry Goulet

In celebration of its fourth anniversary, Valerydesignwrks is proud to offer to its clients and potential clients, for a second year in a row, an environmentally friendly creation. The previous year's calendar was mostly showcasing animal and nature illustrations, this year the illustrations feature humans as main characters. In addition to the calendar, the illustrator's favorite illustrations were also reproduced using the offcuts from the calendar and given as mini prints and greeting cards.

2010 Valerydesignwrks Illustrative Calendar

Dice Calendar

Designer: Syu Makino

This is a dice type calendar and it's possible to use it even in the place where there's space constraints - it being small and handy. For the first half of the year the address side is folded along the dotted line, assembled and made into a dice shape. The latter half of the year - the first half of the year is reversed and it breaks off the page of advertisements along the dotted line. Once again, assemble it into a dice shape and use. The remainders can be recycled as a page of postcard size advertisements.

Client : Hong Kong Polytechnic University
School of Design
Senior Designer: Ken Li

Convert Time to Timeless Ideas

Commissioned to create a small giveaway piece to secondary schools and prospective students as a hand-out on the PolyU Education Info Day 2009 to promote the School of Design. A memorable piece was created to represent the school and the field of design. The calendar was designed to incorporate the school's history as a polytechnic and to function well in Hong Kong culture. Gregorian and Lunar calendars were laid out as if they were markings on a measuring device, allowing comprehensive information to fit into a small form factor. The solution was environmentally friendly and low cost.

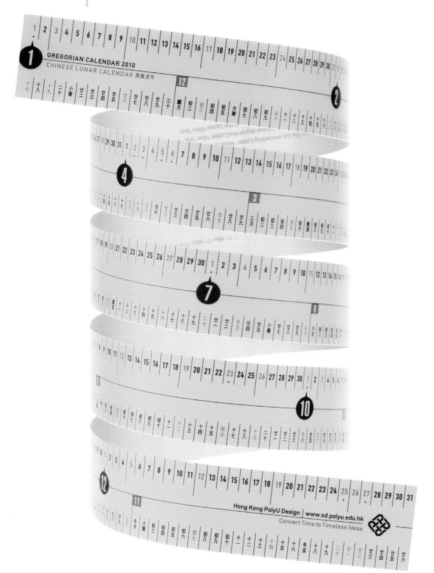

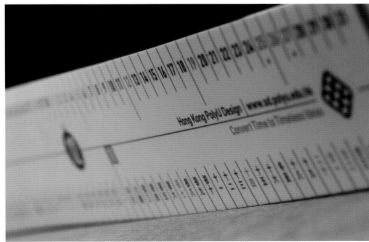

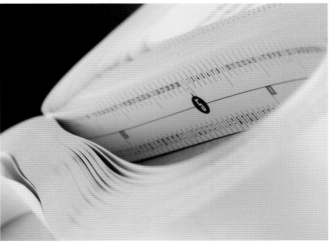

www.airside.co.uk

Every year since its inception, Airside has produced a calendar featuring a selection of illustrations from the past year. As well as showcasing the best of our client-led and self-initiated work, the Airside Calendar also features our favourite non-commissioned pitch ideas and exclusive sketches. 27 brand new illustrations - in bi-weekly intervals, showcasing the respected and rejected Airside work from the past year. Arranged in fortnightly flaps, the 2010 Airside Calendar features a brand new date design with plenty of room for those crucial appointments that you just wouldn't trust to your fancy, gadget-filled phone. As ever, we have strived to make the 2010 Airside Calendar as green as we can. Printed in the UK, the 2010 Airside Calendar comes on FSC-approved recycled paper made from 100% post-consumer waste using bio-vegetable-oil-based inks.

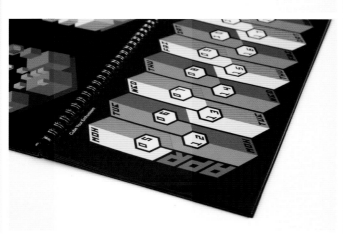

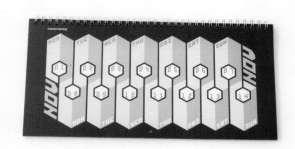
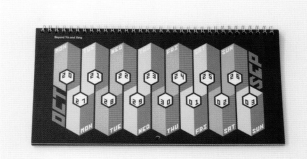

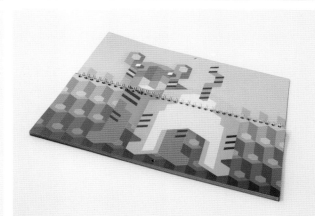

Theaterblut 05

A print diary about theater, opera and dance; a box which contains a folder, a calendar from 11/04 to 03/06, an index, several inlays, 2 sticker sheets, one set of postcards, 3 of 18 different buttons and a DVD. Theaterblut 05 doesn't have a linear structure like normal calendars which allows you to take out what you don't need and put in other things.

Client: Schweizerischer Bühnenverband.
Typeface: NB55RMS, Dove Type Pro.

Client: Schweizerischer Bühnenverband

Theaterblut 06

In its third year, the diary is still built like a construction set or as an open source calendar: you decide how to compose your theatrical year! In this box you'll find everything you need about the theater: a diary from September 2005 to December 2006 with lots of opening night/premiere dates, a filing system, an index, information, addresses, ideas for playing/plays, stickers, postcards, quotes and a theaterblut-patch, to accompany you during a year filled with surprises'.

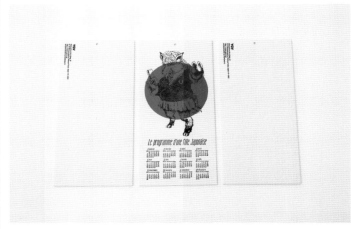

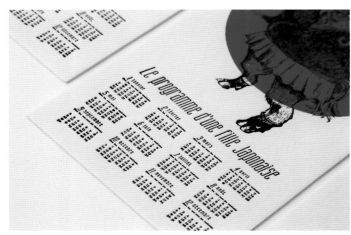

ygv co.ltd | pg
129
www.ygv.jp

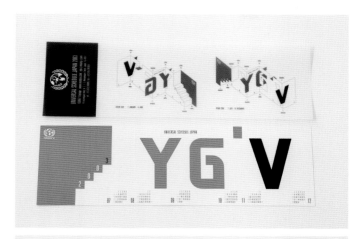

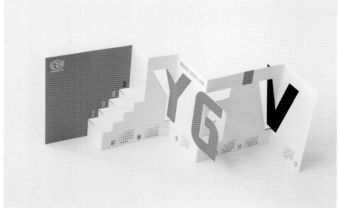

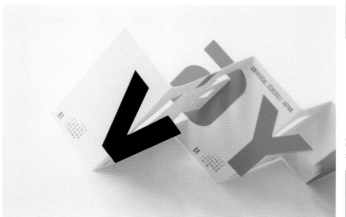

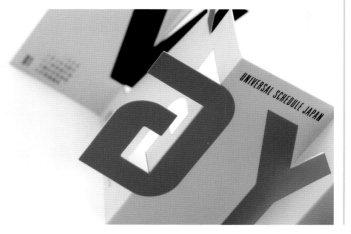

Bicentennial Calendar

The 200-year calendar was designed as a promotional piece for the studio. It was letterpress printed by Studio On Fire, Minneapoli, USA on 600 g/m2 Crane Lettra Pearl White.

Measurement : 420 mm x 297 mm.

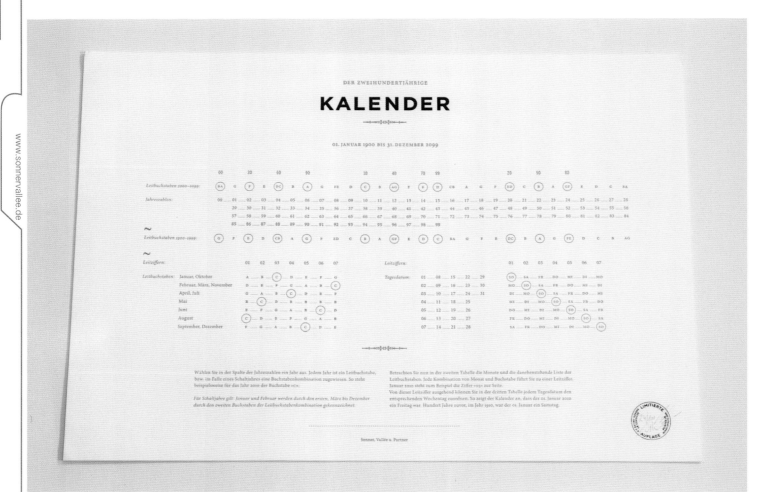

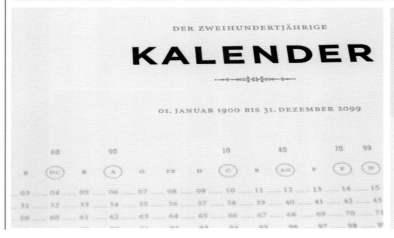

DER ZWEIHUNDERTJÄHRIGE

KALENDER

01. JANUAR 1900 BIS 31. DEZEMBER 2099

Kirkwood 2009

The pages in the calendar are the outcome of a course assignment which had each student from Prof Resnick's junior-level design class create a series of three posters based on themes of ecological responsibility, sustainability, global warming mitigation and environmental stewardship through the conceptualization of 12 assigned keywords. The keywords used were: Reuse, Reduce, Renew, Responsible, Recycle, Rethink, Redesign, Restore, Revise, Reinvent, Respect, Reclaim.

Client: Kirkwood Printing
Design / Production:
Tegan Vacira-Doucet
Caley Ostrander
Olivia Butrick
Elizabeth Resnick, advisor

Students:

Angelica Bonilla	Giovana Lippi	Kimberlie Sanders	Rumiana Williams
Ariele Russell	Jessica Cooke	Kyle Hebert	Ryan Homes
Bryan Paul	Joe Blair	Lia Olsborg	Sarah Smith
Caley Ostrander	Johanna Kenney	Luka Liu	Tegan Vacirca-Doucet
Carlos Troche	Justin Zawilinski	Mark Boroyan	Tian RuFei
Danielle Stanton	Kali Winkler	Olivia Butrick	Yoshiko Doi
Eric Ente	Katie Rezza	Reid Hannan	Erica Sullivan, TA
	Katya Kozlova	Rita Ferreira	Jamie Lee Connor, TA

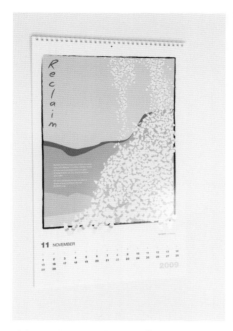

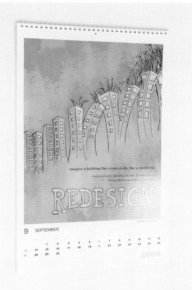

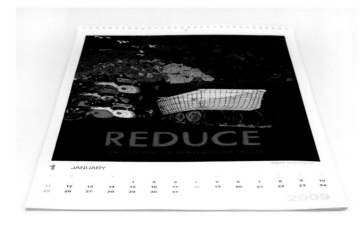

miyuki ueda studio

www.miyuki-ueda.com

The world of Japanese modern

Art with a sense of the different seasons. These pages are filled with encouragement, with energetic pictures and words for the user. Colors like black and gold are the best combinations to express a Japanese 'world'. The calendar is made in the shape of the letter 'A' in reference to the client Arjowiggins K.K.

Client: Arjowiggins K.K.
Art Director: Akihiko Tsukamoto (Zuan Club)
Creative Director: Masami Ouch
Artist: Miyuki Ueda

Henry Wadsworth Longfellow

Symbol of Life – Refresh U Everyday!

Our daily lives are filled with symbols - some of them are essential to our communication, while others help to express our emotions. By using these familiar symbols as the design elements to bring out practical tips, we can make our daily lives more fruitful and positive. ("?": curiosity keeps us going; "+": keep learning build up professional; "=": equality is the essence of harmony; ":)": emotion sharpens your senses, etc.) User-friendly and simplicity are the keywords of the structure. The stand of the calendar is self-adhesive, and the use of multiple colors enhances the mood of "Life is amazing". Last but not least, various kinds of papers (with different thickness, textures and finishing) are used for this calendar, as to match the uniqueness and show the characteristic of each of them, special printing effects like hot-stamping, embossing, luminous ink, spot UV, etc. are applied as well.

Concept & Design: Wicky Lam
Thanks to Antalis (HK) for providing the actual calendar.

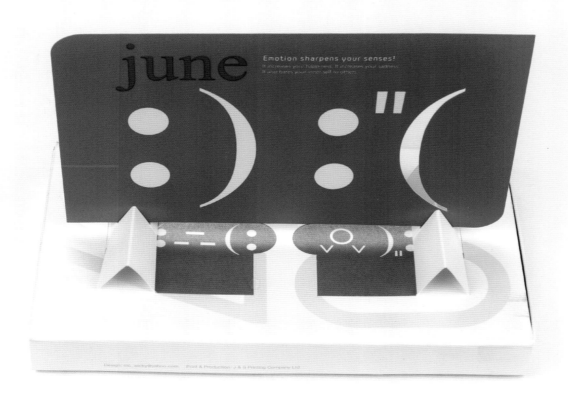

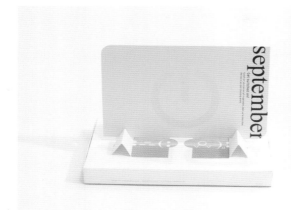

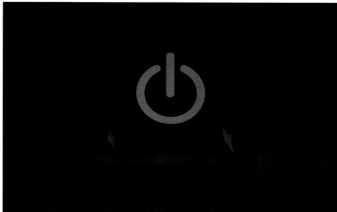

Antalis Calendar 2009

It's a cute miniature of a pallet of printed sheets – the most typical of what you can see at printing workshops. The wooden pallet was made with reference to the real thing. The page layout of the calendar is to mimic a magazine printed sheet. 365 sheets contain 365 days of a year being stacked up on 3 wooden pallet boards (4 months in a pile) one arranged on top of another. A small batch of sticker notes is enclosed for users to make remarks on important days as they use them. The outcome will look exactly like a pile of printed sheets on which pressmen have marked advances.

Design Director: Eddy Yu, Hung Lam
Designer: Christy Chen
Photographer: Kwan Kai Wing (glossmatt), Hung Lam
Copy Writer: Alice Lee, Christy Chen
Printer: Willey Printing & Production Ltd.
Client: Antalis (HK) Ltd.
Thanks to Antalis (HK) for providing the actual calendar.

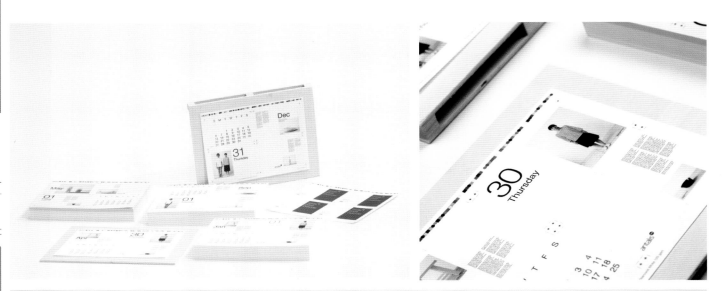

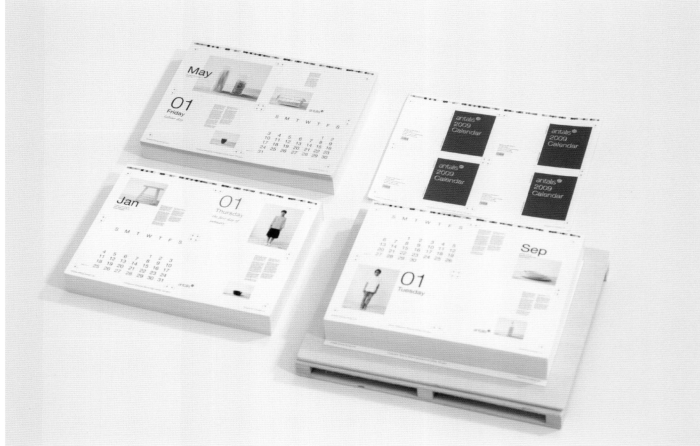

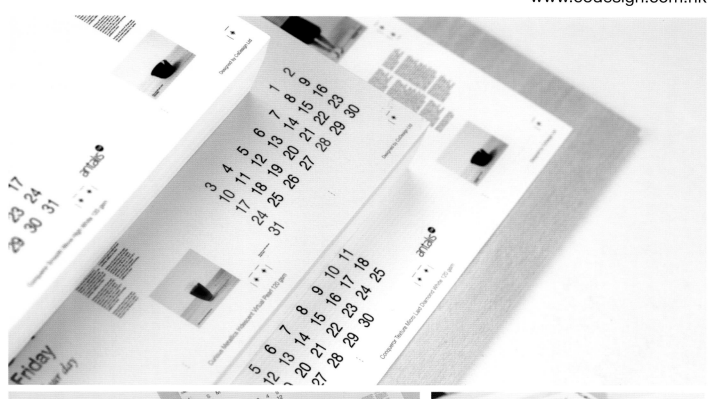

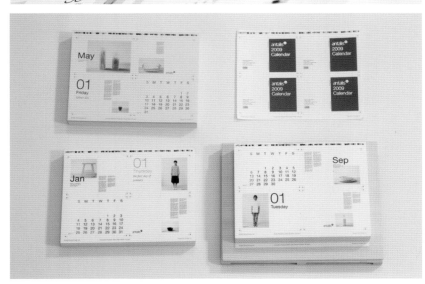

Calendar 2009

A calendar where every weekday is given its own colour to simplify navigation around the calendar.

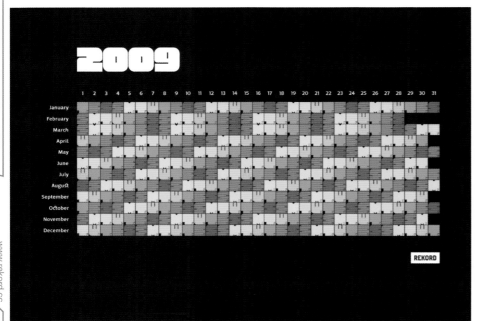

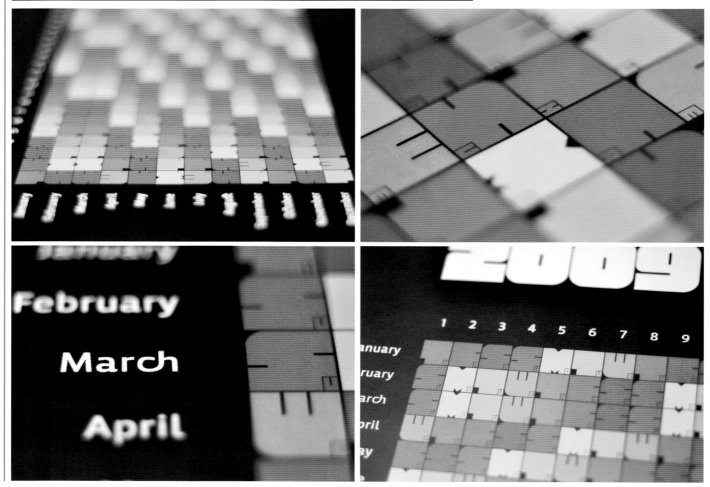

Calendar 2010

A calendar which is designed to save space: as you unfold it into an A3 size, you can also fold it back into a monthly strip.

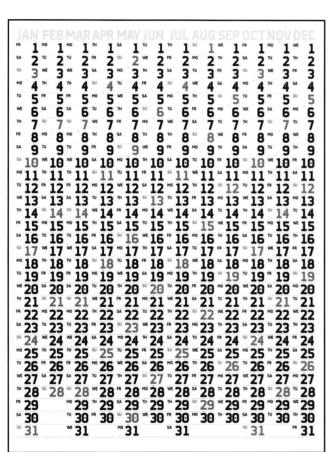

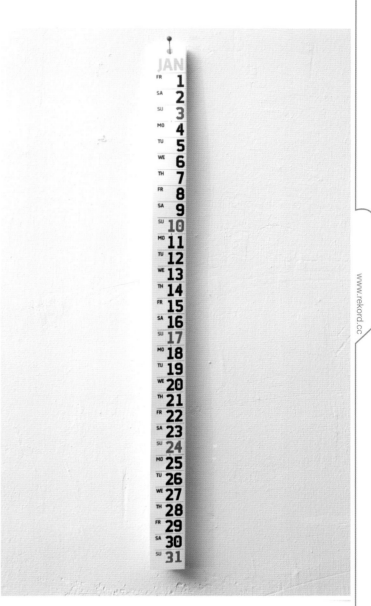

12x12 Design Calendar

2x12 is a calendar made by 12 graphic designers: Marc Karpstein, Kriš Salmanis, Shiho Kikuchi, Yoshihiro Yoshida, Monika Grūzīte, Kirils Kirasirovs, Mārtiņš Ratniks, Anete Melece, Dirk Laucke, Sandijs Ruļuks, Zigmunds Lapsa, Liene Drāzniece. It is silkscreen printed in limited edition of 150 pieces, each is numbered.

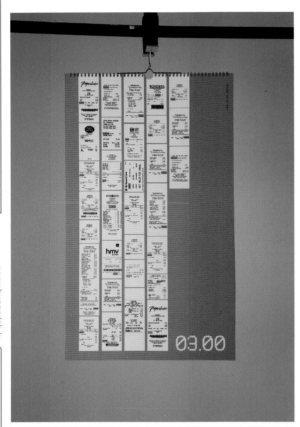

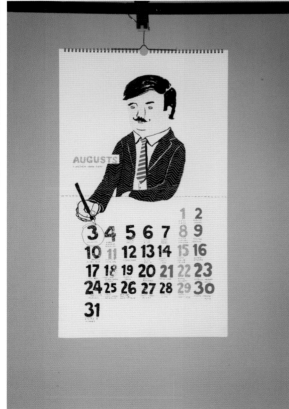

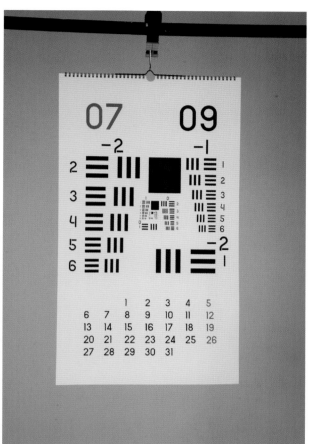

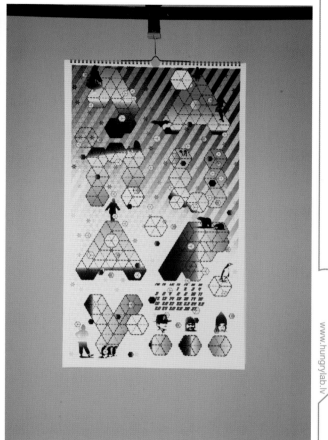

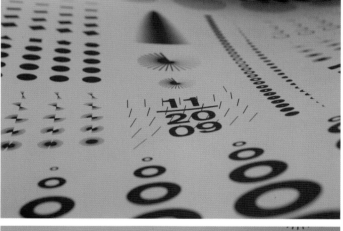

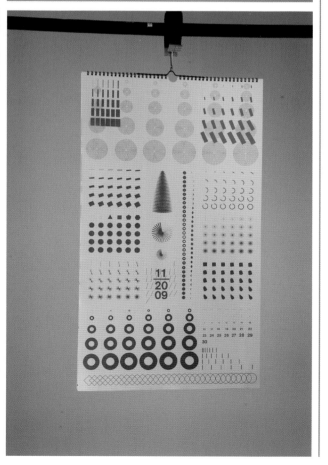

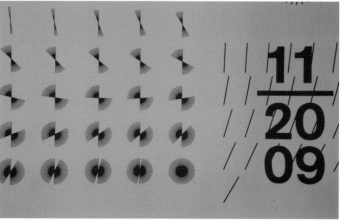

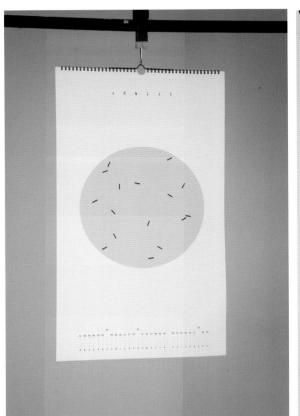

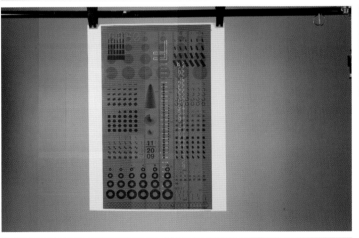

Designer: Valerie Thai

The Cabin + Cub calendar

The Cabin + Cub calendar features 12 mixed media collage images to brighten your days! Each calendar comes with 12 different individual cards (one for each month) printed with Ultrachrome K3 archival inks on heavy rich archival matte paper. Each calendar also includes a reusable wooden mini easel stand.

Dimensions: each card is 4 x 5.25 inches.

Calendar of 2010

There's not a street in the world that does not have its own special look. Shaped by the appearance of the stores and brands, and the people to whom these shops appeal to, namely the particular target group. Using the appropriate visual identity is the best way to appeal to prospective clients - in an eye-catching and focused way. ROSAGELB creates such visual identities that are always tailored to the target group, always with a genuine feel, and always coherent. Incidentally: ROSAGELB also collaborates with outstanding sign-makers.

ROSAGELB
PINKYELLOW
ROSAAMARILLO
黄玫瑰

Visuelle Identität
Visual identity
视觉形象设计
Identidad visual

Elbestr. 10
60329 Frankfurt
Germany

T. +49 (0)69 48 44 82 96
E. studio@rosagelb.de
www.rosagelb.de

© 2010 ROSAGELB

Jeder Zielgruppe ihr Erscheinungsbild

Alle Straßen auf der Welt haben ihren speziellen Look. Geprägt wird dieser vom Erscheinungsbild der Läden und Marken dort und von den Menschen, die von diesen Geschäften angesprochen werden – der spezifischen Zielgruppe.

Deren prägnante und fokussierte Ansprache geschieht über das passende Erscheinungsbild. ROSAGELB schafft solche Erscheinungsbilder. Immer zielgruppengerecht, immer authentisch, immer identitätsstiftend.

Übrigens: ROSAGELB arbeitet auch mit hervorragenden Schildermachern zusammen.

目标客户群及其特有形象

世界上每一条街道都有其独特的形象，它来自于那里的店、品牌以及喜欢在那儿逛这些商店的人 – 他们就是目标客户群。

一目了然，清晰无误是描绘这种形象的准则。黄玫瑰就能做到这一点。总是瞄准看目标客户，总是可靠，总是符合身份。

还有一点很重要：黄玫瑰还与优秀的招牌制作人合作。

The right identity for the particular target group

There's not a street in the world that does not have its own special look. Shaped by the appearance of the stores and brands, and the people to whom these shops appeal to, namely the particular target group.

Using the appropriate visual identity is the best way to appeal to prospective clients – in an eye-catching and focused way. PINKYELLOW creates such visual identities that are always tailored to the target group, always with a genuine feel, and always coherent.

Incidentally: PINKYELLOW also collaborates with outstanding sign-makers.

La identidad adecuada para el grupo target especifico

No hay una sola calle en el mundo que no tenga su propia personalidad, definida por el aspecto de las tiendas y las marcas, y por la gente a la que estas tiendas atraen, es decir, el grupo objetivo específico.

La utilización de la identidad visual adecuada es la mejor manera de atraer potenciales clientes... de forma llamativa y definida. ROSAAMARILLO crea identidades visuales dirigidas claramente al grupo objetivo, con un mensaje siempre genuino y coherente.

A propósito: ROSAAMARILLO también colabora con rotulistas de primer orden.

20 10

Januar / January / 一月 / Enero — 2010

	4	11	18	25
	5	12	19	26
	6	13	20	27
	7	14	21	28
1	8	15	22	29
2	9	16	23	30
3	10	17	24	31

Goethestraße Frankfurt · 法兰克福歌德街 · Frankfurt Goethe Street · Calle Goethe Frankfurt

Februar / February / 二月 / Febrero — 2010

1	8	15	22
2	9	16	23
3	10	17	24
4	11	18	25
5	12	19	26
6	13	20	27
7	14	21	28

Münchner Straße Frankfurt · 法兰克福慕尼黑街 · Frankfurt Munich Street · Calle Munich Frankfurt

März / March / 三月 / Marzo — 2010

1	8	15	22	29
2	9	16	23	30
3	10	17	24	31
4	11	18	25	
5	12	19	26	
6	13	20	27	
7	14	21	28	

Berger Straße Frankfurt · 法兰克福贝格尔街 · Frankfurt Berger Street · Calle Berger Frankfurt

April / April / 四月 / Abril — 2010

	5	12	19	26
	6	13	20	27
	7	14	21	28
1	8	15	22	29
2	9	16	23	30
3	10	17	24	
4	11	18	25	

Altstadt Shanghai · 上海旧城 · Shanghai Old City · Casco Viejo Shanghai

Mai / May / 五月 / Mayo — 2010

	3	10	17	24	31
	4	11	18	25	
	5	12	19	26	
	6	13	20	27	
	7	14	21	28	
1	8	15	22	29	
2	9	16	23	30	

Lanxing Weg Guangzhou · 广州栏里 · Guangzhou Lanxing Lane · Calle Lanxing Guangzhou

Juni / June / 六月 / Junio — 2010

	7	14	21	28
1	8	15	22	29
2	9	16	23	30
3	10	17	24	
4	11	18	25	
5	12	19	26	
6	13	20	27	

Beijing Straße Guangzhou · 广州北京街 · Guangzhou Beijing Street · Calle Beijing Guangzhou

Juli / July / 七月 / Julio — 2010

	5	12	19	26
	6	13	20	27
	7	14	21	28
1	8	15	22	29
2	9	16	23	30
3	10	17	24	31
4	11	18	25	

Poble Sec Viertel Barcelona · 巴塞罗那帕布雷塞区 · Barcelona Poble Sec District · Barrio Pueblo Seco Barcelona

August / August / 八月 / Agosto — 2010

	2	9	16	23	30
	3	10	17	24	31
	4	11	18	25	
	5	12	19	26	
	6	13	20	27	
	7	14	21	28	
1	8	15	22	29	

Les Ramblas Barcelona · 巴塞罗那拉布拉斯大道 · Barcelona Les Ramblas · Las Ramblas Barcelona

September / September / 九月 / Septiembre — 2010

	6	13	20	27
	7	14	21	28
1	8	15	22	29
2	9	16	23	30
3	10	17	24	
4	11	18	25	
5	12	19	26	

Sant Pau Straße Barcelona · 巴塞罗那圣保罗街 · Barcelona Sant Pau Street · Calle de San Pablo Barcelona

Oktober / October / 十月 / Octubre — 2010

	4	11	18	25
	5	12	19	26
	6	13	20	27
	7	14	21	28
1	8	15	22	29
2	9	16	23	30
3	10	17	24	31

Regent Straße London · 伦敦摄政街 · London Regent Street · Calle Regent Londres

November / November / 十一月 / Noviembre — 2010

1	8	15	22	29
2	9	16	23	30
3	10	17	24	
4	11	18	25	
5	12	19	26	
6	13	20	27	
7	14	21	28	

Chinatown London · 伦敦中国城 · London Chinatown · Barrio Chino Londres

ROSAGELB
PINKYELLOW
ROSAAMARILLO
黄玫瑰

Visuelle Identität
Visual Identity
视觉形象设计
Identidad visual

Elbestr. 10
60329 Frankfurt
Germany

T. +49. (0)69. 48 48 62 96
E. studio@rosagelb.com
www.rosagelb.de

Calend-art

These were all part of a project in which our design team were given a brief to create a really cool piece of artwork that also doubled as a calendar. They were screen-printed as limited edition runs of 100 or less and sent to our valued clients. They quickly became collectable. Shane Hansen and Johnson McKay were both involved in this project.

January: Meanwhile down at the water coolerof life...
- Shane Hansen aka 'Fly on Wall'
February: The big F - Tim Hansen
March: March of the voodoo zombies
- Steve Kitchen (Combination 13)
April: Oh my sweet april
- Steve Kitchen (Combination 13)
July: The winter blues are brewin' - Abhi Rajkumar

Acupuncture Calendar

We were tasked to develop an unusual advertising campaign for current patients and business partners of an acupuncture practice. Acupuncture works with 360 acupuncture points. We illustrated this with an innovative calendar: each day of the month corresponds to an acupuncture point, which the user can mark with a needle. The twelve pages of the calendar represent different areas of the body, each highlighting relevant acupuncture points. The special feature is the porous texture of the paper which mimics the feel of human skin. This further boosts the effect of the images. An advertising campaign to increase the loyalty of the target group to the acupuncture practice and keep the topic of traditional Chinese medicine in people's minds for a whole year.

Overall, the target group was very impressed by the design of the calendar, especially the texture of the paper and the oversized depictions of body parts and acupuncture points.

Client: Practice for Traditional Chinese
Medicine - DR.MED.
Ralph-Peter Schink,
DR.MED. Werner Jansen.
Executive Creative Director: Wolf Heumann
Creative Director: Ove Gley
Art Director: Lars Borker
Graphic Design: Daniel Such, Nives Teskera
Photographer: Timo Kerber

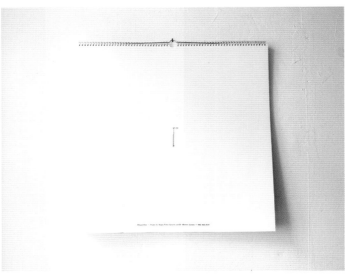

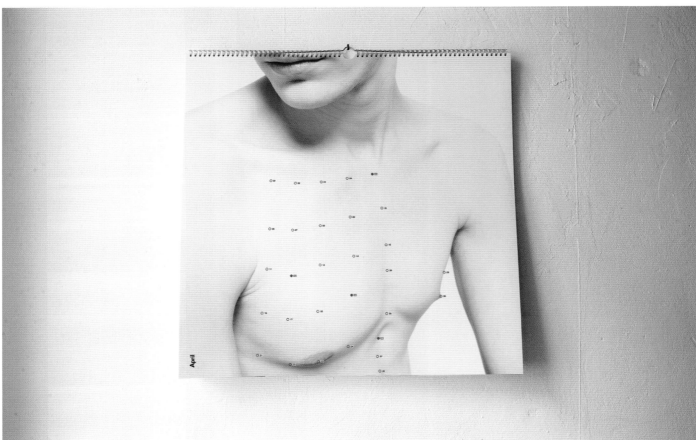

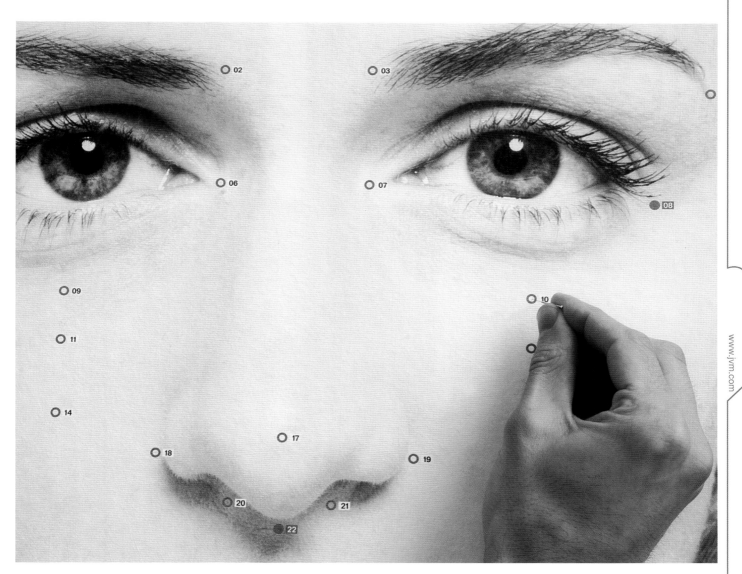

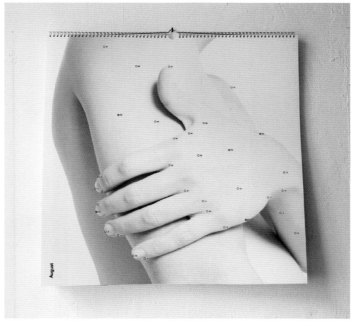

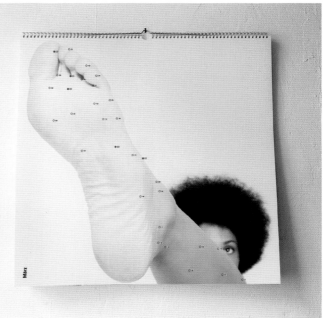

The 2010 agenda for La Casa Encendida

La Casa Encendida is a social and cultural center in Madrid that hosts a variety of contemporary artistic presentations and educational activities. We designed a multitasking agenda with a plastic jacket to hold leaflets, pens, business cards, and a La Casa CD. Every spread contains a color gradient based on data of daily temperatures and hours of daylight in Madrid throughout the year.

design project
www.designproject.co.uk

Sirio 09

Client: Fedrigoni UK

Briefed by Fedrigoni UK to create a practical yet design-led desk object, Design Project responded by producing a calendar that is both functional and beautiful. The design features week-to-view flip-up cards in a colour co-ordinated sequence, promoting Fedrigoni's Sirio range of coloured paper and board. The project also involved creating a bespoke numerals typeface, designed to enable easy day-to-day navigation.

Dimensions: 90 x 140 mm

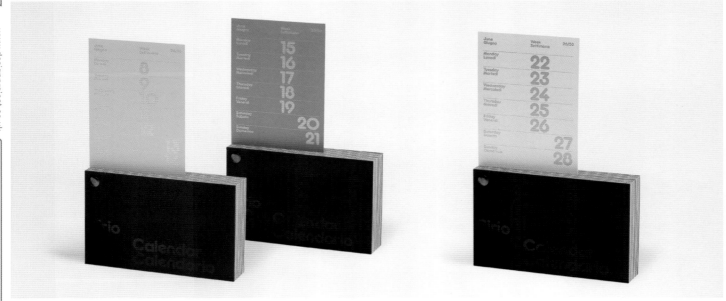

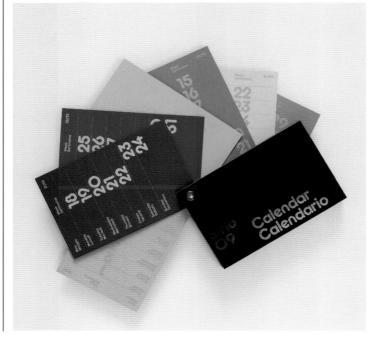

Concept: Liquan Liew & Fanny Khoo
Creative Director: Fanny Khoo
Designers:

January	How to start the new year (By Adeline Tan)
February	How to love (By Tom Merckx)
March	How to communicate better (By Chi Ying Chung)
April	How to be funny (By Liquan Liew)
May	How to work better (By Liquan Liew)
June	How to plan for the perfect holiday (By Shinta Wijaya)
July	How to organize better (By Adeline Tan)
August	How to behave (By Tom Merckx)
September	How to eat (By Liquan Liew)
October	How to save money better (By Chi Ying Chung)
November	How to sleep better (By Kristal Melson)
December	How to feel better (By Kristal Melson)

Print: Colourscan in Singapore

Equus & RJ Limited Edition Wall Calendar

This massive wall calendar is a labour of love shared by six designers, put together for RJ papers as their premium giveaway for the holiday season. Designed around the concept of HOW-TO infographics, each poster is unique in flavor and style. The project was set up by Equus in Singapore.

Paper: RJ papers Dimensions: A1

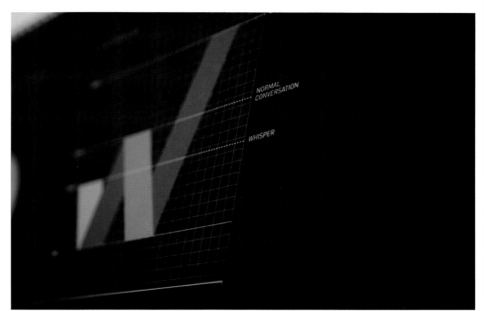

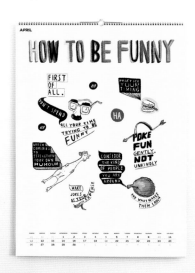

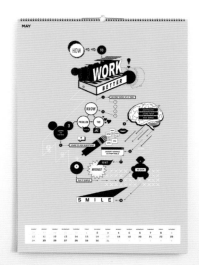

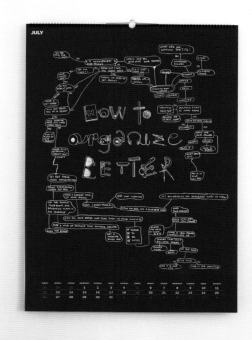

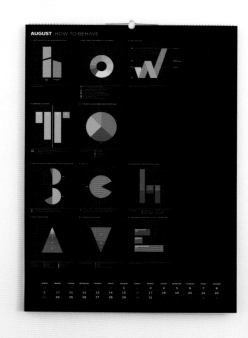

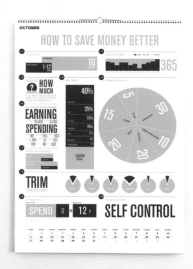

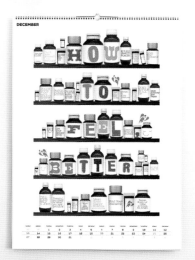

Jagda Calendar Salone 2011

This work is in an almanac typography, the meaning of which you can´t discover until you look and feel with care. Like TIME itself, it doesn´t exist until you find it.

Client: Jagda Calendar Salone 2011
Art Director: Haruhiko Taniuchi
Director: Haruhiko Taniuchi, Sho Oyama

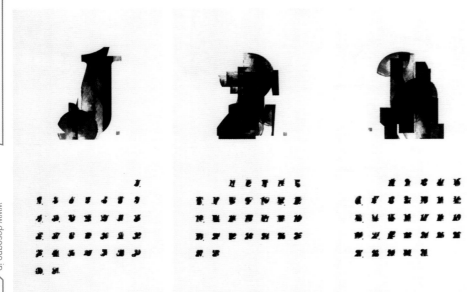

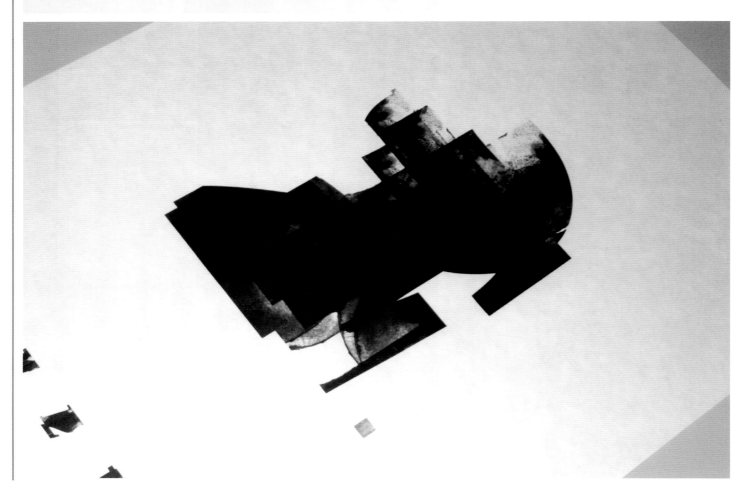

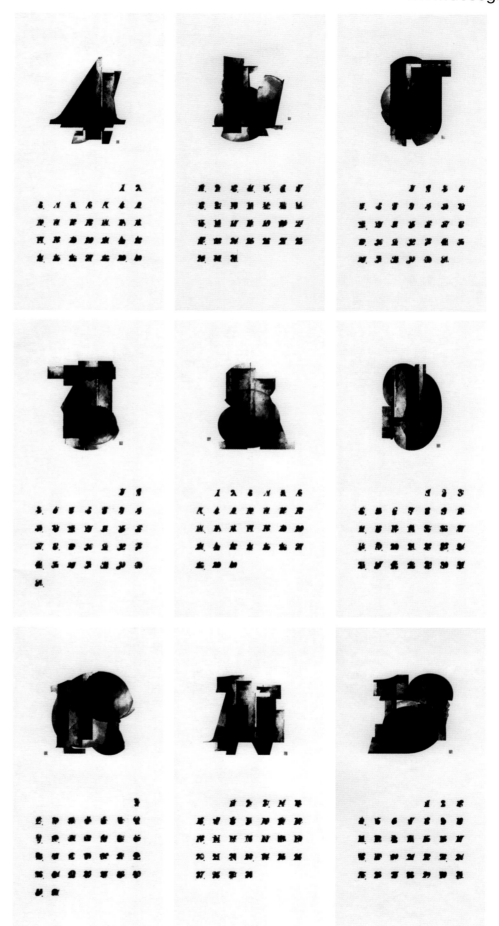

studio8 design
www.studio8design.co.uk

Fedrigoni 2010 Calendar

A post-it style calendar, for Italian paper company Fedrigoni, with a page-per-day, one color per month and perforated fold-up numbers.

Client: Fedrigoni
Creative Director / Designer: Zoë Bather, Matt Willey

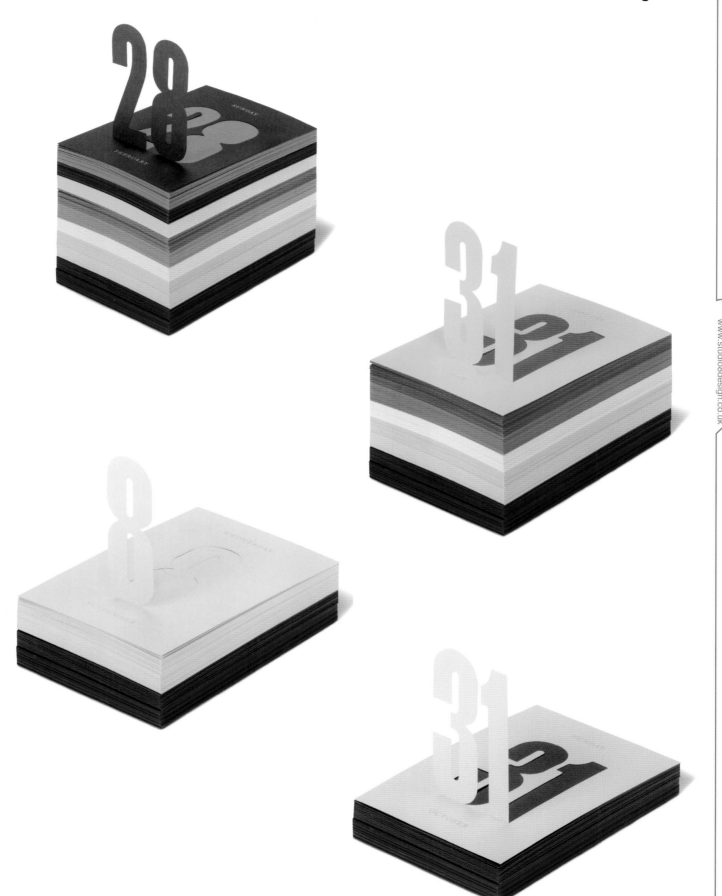

www.andreklauser.com

Date Ruler

A ruler and a calendar used to be two common tools around the workplace. Today most measuring takes place within the applications of our computer and of course this is where we will find a calendar, too. The Date Ruler combines two seemingly obsolete tools in one object, simply by adding 1 centimetre and 2 magnetic markers to an otherwise standard steel ruler. The same increments now measure both time and distance. There is a curious attraction in combining the 2 objects which partly drives this proposal. But there is another motivation behind the design, which is to give new relevance to a physical representation of the functions of telling time and measuring distance. The object says that it is good to have a dedicated object in a specific place that we can turn to if we want to know what the date is. And it says that it is good to have a physical object around that can give us a true sense of scale.

Dimensions: 3.2 × 35cm

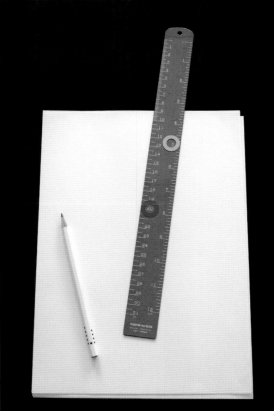
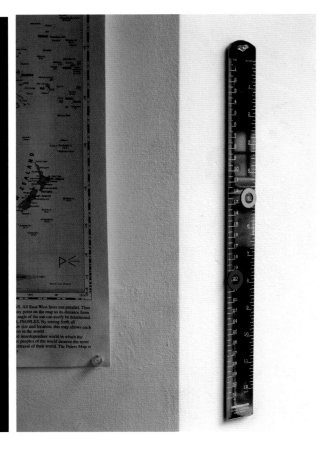

Calendar 2009

This design features brown paper / card stock and white (silk screened) ink.

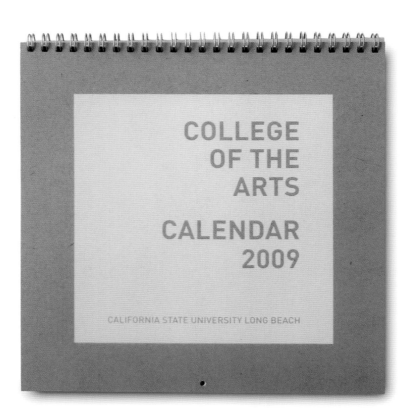

art. lebedev studio

www.artlebedev.com

Tetra Pak 2010 Calendar

Tetra Pak does a good job of keeping food and drinks fresh—they produce nice and durable packaging. Their 2010 calendar shows how various kinds of cartons and boxes are created.

Client: Tetra Pak
Art director: Oleg Pashchenko
Designer / Imposer: Vladimir Zotov
Designer / Photographer: Anna Ponomaryova
Designer: Constantin Dolzhenko
Editor: Philipp Shprints
Manager: Marina Tolstokorova

Январь January

Tetra Rex

Пик свежести

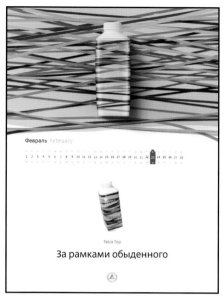

Февраль February

Tetra Top

За рамками обыденного

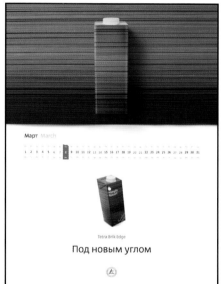

Март March

Tetra Brik Edge

Под новым углом

Апрель April

Tetra Classic Aseptic

На радость всем

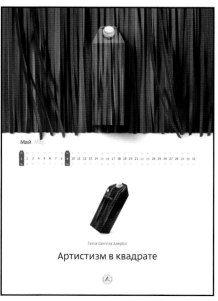

Май May

Tetra Gemina Aseptic

Артистизм в квадрате

Июнь June

Tetra Prisma Aseptic

Обращение к чувствам

Июль July

Tetra Brik Aseptic

Просто гениально

Август August

Tetra Fino Aseptic

Безупречная простота

Сентябрь September

1 2 3 4 5 6 7 8 9 10 11 12 13 14 15 16 17 18 19 20 21 22 23 24 25 26 27 28 29 30

Tetra Wedge Aseptic

Игривое настроение

Октябрь October

Tetra Recart

Альтернатива 21-го века

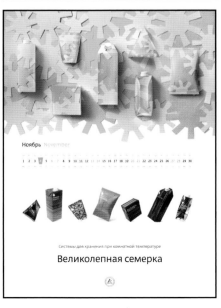

Ноябрь November

Системы для хранения при комнатной температуре

Великолепная семерка

Декабрь December

Системы для холодного хранения

Снежная тройка

Year of Astronomy - The Papercy Project

Technology is cyclical. Old processes can become new again. As creators, we do not have to be so caught up in the blind chase for the latest technologies. Any technique that can be employed to enhance an end-product should be harnessed. It is more important to develop a sensitivity towards the design medium. The aim behind this calendar design was to make the outcome more interesting and less "flat" by augmenting digital prints (laser jet and deskjet) with handicraft methods (letterpress, silkscreen, varnish, die-cut, emboss, etc.) and different textures of paper with overlays (which can be switched around for different compositions). The calendar portion is also perforated and can be torn away for the designs to be kept as posters. It would have been rather cliche to base the designs on horoscopes, because the theme of the calendar is Astronomy after all. Instead, I created a series of general designs based on the theme. Similarly, a calendar was chosen because it gives more context as a functional design outcome rather than just a poster series. All these steps were taken in an effort to enhance the graphic design outcome for both creatives and end-users alike.

Dimensions: 297 x 520 mm

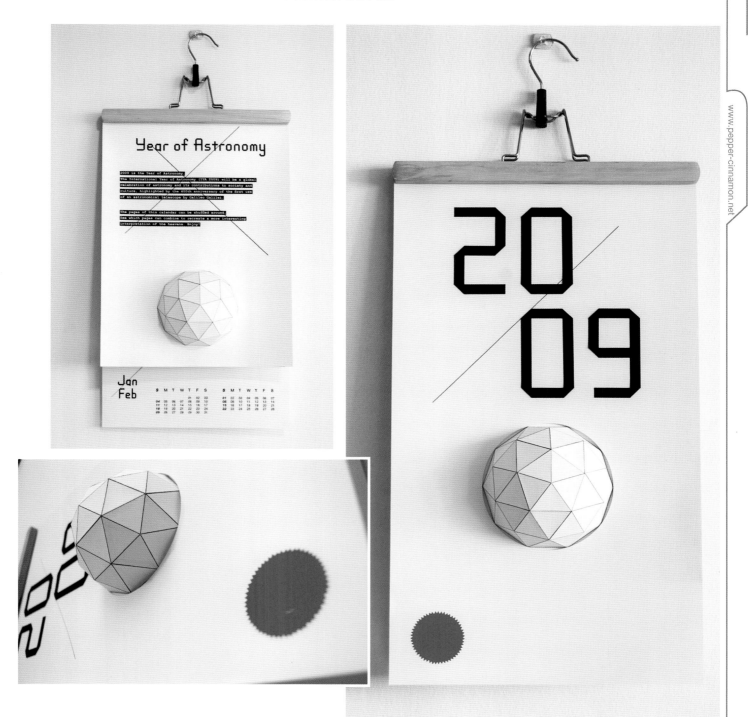

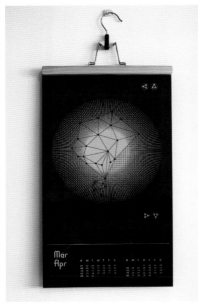

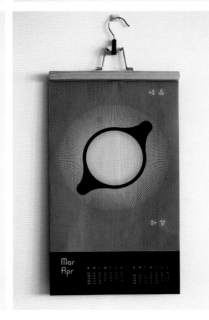

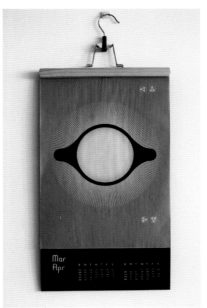

Bubble Calendar

"Popping bubbles is something everyone loves," says Stephen Turbek, designer of the Bubble Calendar, explaining the inspiration behind the design. "Kids love learning about the calendar while popping the bubbles. Bubble Calendar is also the perfect gift for that obsessive person in your life; as long as they don't pop the whole year the first day!" The calendar is fully functional, with days of the week and all major U.S. holidays marked and weekends in bold for easy reference - available with either a thick paper or clear plastic backing.

Dimensions: 48 x 18"

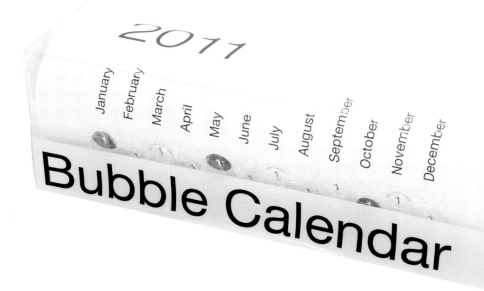

Copyright 2008-2011 Bubble Calendar LLC   Designed in Brooklyn, Made in China

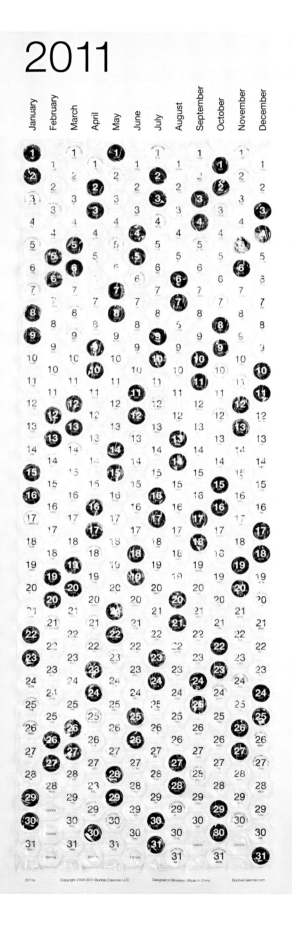

chris haughton
www.vegetablefriedrice.com

People Tree Calendar

People tree (www.peopletree.co.uk) is a fairtrade clothing network of very small cooperatives and projects all over the world - about 70 or 80 fairly small sized producer groups ranging from 10 to 150 full or part-time workers in 20 different countries. They work in the least developed areas of the poorest countries mainly setting up projects based on the locally handicrafts, they make handmade paper notepads and cards in nepal, hand-knitted alpaca wool products in peru, t-shirts made from local subsistence cotton farmer's cotton in India. All of these small groups are then able to sell their products worldwide through people tree on the people tree site. It's such a simple idea and the network cuts out the middle-man and helps the really poorest areas build a way out of poverty. Many of the producer groups and projects are set up to employ either women who have been victims of domestic abuse or disabled individuals who would not be able to earn money outside of their family.

april

mon	tue	wed	thu	fri	sat	sun
			1	2	3	4
5	6	7	8	9	10	11
12	13	14	15	16	17	18
19	20	21	22	23	24	25
26	27	28	29	30		

www.peopletree.co.uk

april

mon	tue	wed	thu	fri	sat	sun
	1	2	3	4	5	6
7	8	9	10	11	12	13
14	15	16	17	18	19	20
21	22	23	24	25	26	27
28	29	30				

www.peopletree.co.uk

February

mon	tue	wed	thu	fri	sat	sun
1	2	3	4	5	6	7
8	9	10	11	12	13	14
15	16	17	18	19	20	21
22	23	24	25	26	27	28

www.peopletree.co.uk

march

mon	tue	wed	thu	fri	sat	sun
					1	2
3	4	5	6	7	8	9
10	11	12	13	14	15	16
17	18	19	20	21	22	23
24	25	26	27	28	29	30
31						

ire only

www.peopletree.co.uk

Customizable Agenda (Utrecht School of Arts 2005)

Products developed by graphic designers usually serve their purpose for a limited time. Sometimes the project deals with time as such, for example agendas, calendars, annual reports or your typical graphic design projects. In order to present the usually deadly dull information in course catalogue in a more accessible way, the HKU wanted to produce an agenda for students in which all the regulations, schedules, opening hours, addresses and other small-print items would be included. The agenda begins and ends with 16 pages of stickers bearing important reminders such as , birthday, party, beer, exams, etc., which the user can use to customize his or her agenda. The exuberant design is based on a set of simple rules for combining seven colors, seven shapes and seven patterns. As these were mixed consistently, no two spreads are alike and yet the publication remains a unified whole.

de designpolitie | pg
175
www.designpolitie.nl

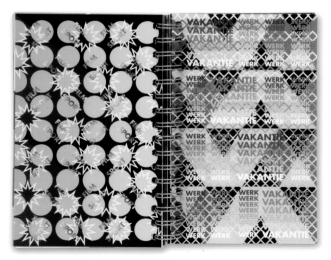

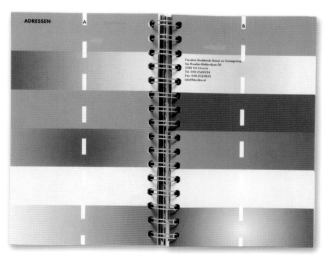

www.c-p-u.co.jp

Creative Power Unit Calendar

Dimensions: 275 x 95mm (folded)

Art Director: Tatsushi Nagae
Designer: Daisuke Katayama

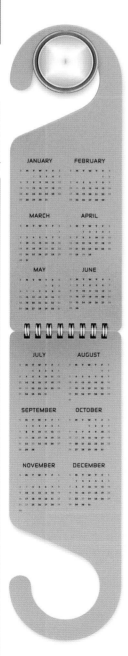

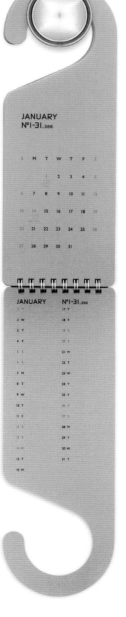

Client: Spinhex & Industrie Drukkerij

2006-4704-5766-1427

The calendar integrates the four most commonly used calendar systems, namely, Gregorian, Jewish, Arabic and Chinese, showing the differences / similarities between them. The calendar 'questions' time as a strange and relative concept due to its various ways of measuring. A form of absurdity is presented concerning our perception of time. Months, weeks, days and even hours are measured differently in each system. It consists of four levels - containing its own specific information. Front of the calendar shows the Gregorian system and turning the calendar around, it presents the four different calendar systems parallel to each other. Opening the calendar pages reveals the position of constellations relative to each month, and the seconds, minutes and hours passed each day, for each calendar system. Tearing off the days along the perforations, one is made aware of how much time has passed. The last pages of the calendar contain additional information concerning time measurement. The calendar is printed in full color and uses a UV spot varnish and is printed on paper coated with an emerald finish. The complete calendar is perforated using both a 'stamp' and a 'micro' perforation.

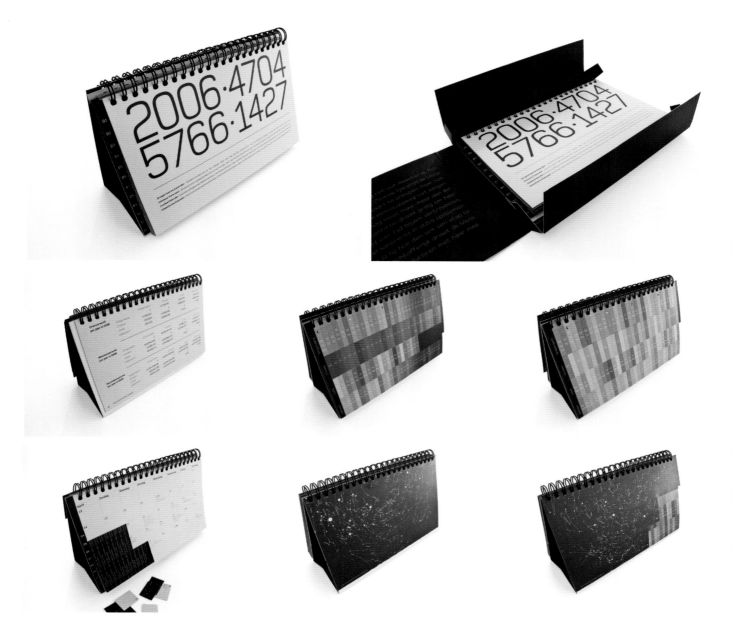

clever⁰ franke

www.cleverfranke.com

Weather Chart 2009

The poster is a visualization of all the weather details for the year 2009. In both graphic and numerical representation, one can read the temperature, precipitation, sunshine, sun rise and sunset times, wind force and direction. Besides a factual representation, we tried to visualize the data in such a way so as to create an intriguing overall image of an every day discussion topic: the weather. The calendar poster is printed in 4 fluorescent and metallic pantone colours and a UV spot varnish.

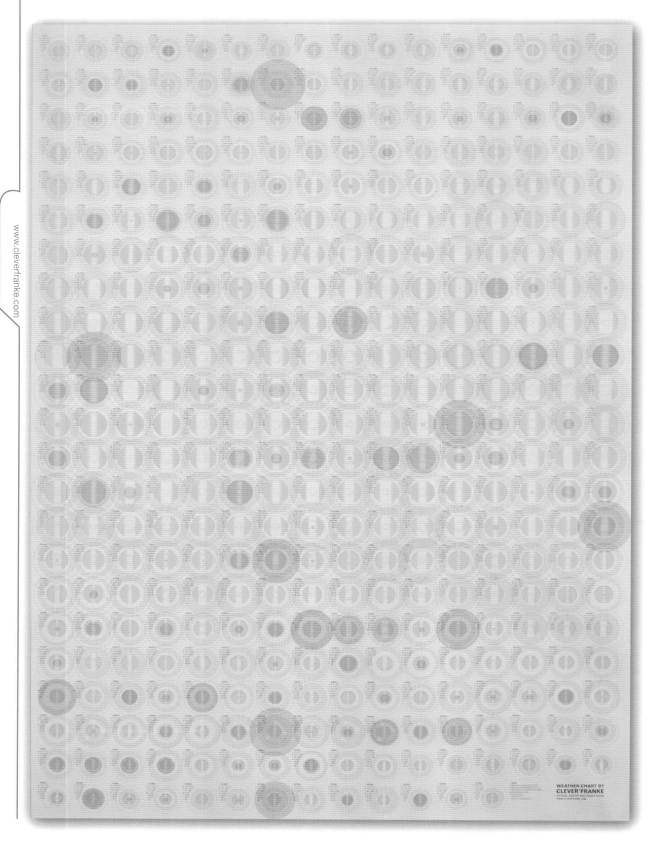

WEATHER CHART BY
CLEVER°FRANKE

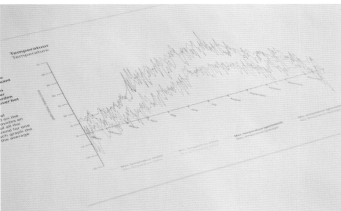

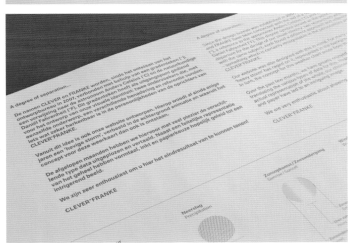

Calendar/Announcement Card

The idea for this self-promotion project is to communicate our existence and arrival to Singapore from New York City, playing on our name "Foreign Policy" and blending concepts of current affairs, political affairs, maps, the world and the leaders. We wanted to do something unconventional, so we mapped the calendar into a world map. The challenge is to make this as intuitive as possible and have people getting used to learn a new 'system'. We even brought in people to have them sit or stand in front of the calendar and ask/test them if they know or understand what it really is. The kit is made up of three components: the calendar, announcement card and the label.

Dimensions: 25 x 21" x 2 sheets + a card

Creative Direction / Art Direction: Yah-Leng Yu, Arthur Chin
Design: Tianyu Isaiah Zheng (TY)
Copywriting: Arthur Chin
Print: pH Productions
Type: Bauer Bodoni, Trade Gothic Condensed

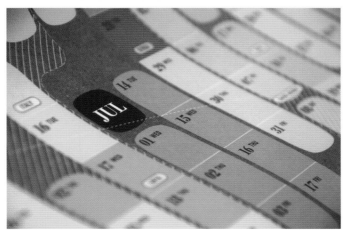

Calendrier

Every year I work with friends on a calendar and the theme is fixed by one of the twelve collaborators.

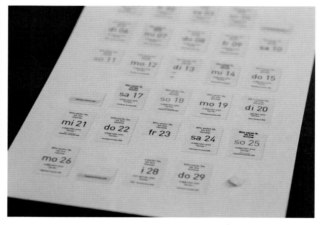

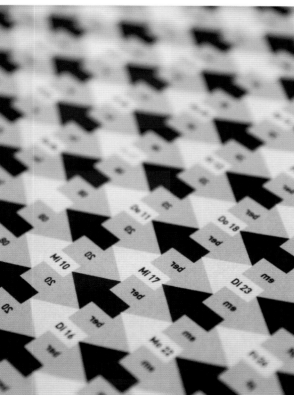

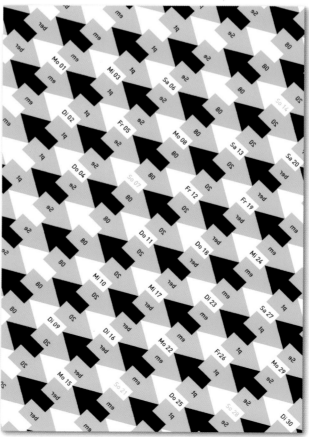

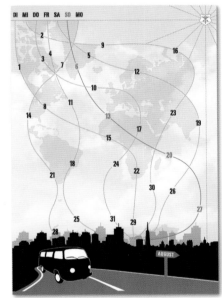

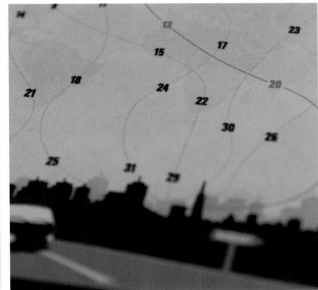

Typographic Keyboard Wall Calendar

It's made of two thousand and ten keyboard keys. This design offers a new visual experience of time, different to your average wall calendar. It looks beautiful on the wall, and makes finding dates and marking events a creative process. The is about the act of notating time in order to organize it. While calendars nowadays are typically used to optimize personal potential by marking events and managing interaction with others, this calendar offers a view on the managing of time itself.

Dimensions: 70 x 100 cm

Happy and Sweet 2009

A corporate gift from Kanella's design studio, designed to wish my clients a Happy New Year. Since it was Kanella design studio's first birthday, I thought of creating something smart, discreet, personal and durable (throughout the year), pleasing to my clients. A box set of 12 chocolates, after the 12 months of the year, each with a different illustration that incorporates an element characteristic of the month (like a rose for Valentine's Day in February). It works as a calendar and the chocolate has to be eaten at the end of each month.

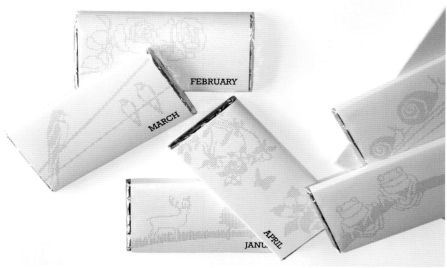

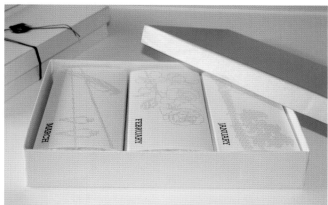

pg
186 | circle-d

www.circle-d.me

Kanji Calendar

This is a calendar with a Kanji motif. A challenge was faced on how far a scene can be described by just using letters. It is silk screen hand-printed. The transparency of the blue color of Mt. Fuji and the word under it was done with extra care.

Client: JAGDA(Japan Graphic Designers Association Inc.)
Art Director / Designer: Masataka Maruyama

Client: JAGDA(Japan Graphic Designers
Association Inc.)
Art Director / Designer: Masataka Maruyama

Timeline Scratch

The dates are scratch type. By scratching out the dates, we can appreciate each and every day. We hope that every day will turn into a precious memory. The whole page is in scratch print in this calendar in order to feel time flying by.

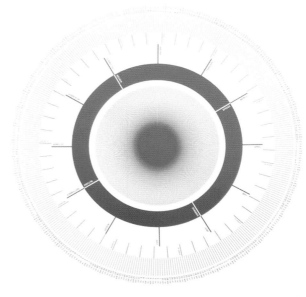

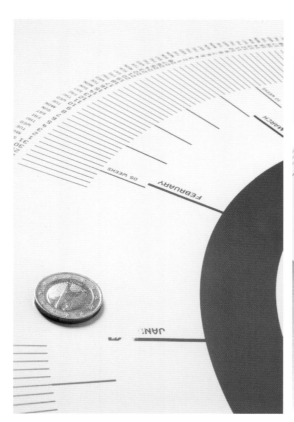

National properties are a good topic, because they are important and memorable assets in the country and also they have their own month/time of origin or period of activity. The concept or content of this calendar is National properties (monuments / treasures) in South Korea. In this calendar, vector images show the features of each National property and place them on each relevant month (for their time of origin, period of activity). Focussing on the shape of National properties - geometric forms that support the graphics. Besides basic calendar information, there is information about each month's featured property.

Dimensions: 297 x 420 mm

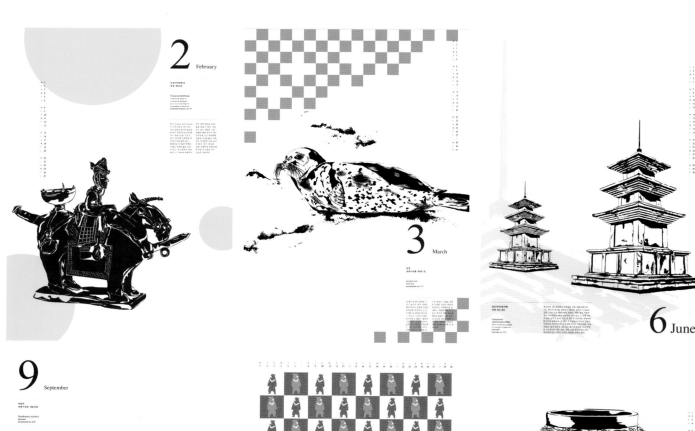

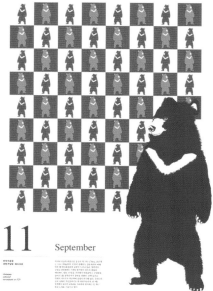

Designer: Ryan Yoon and Harc Lee

4 Seasons Calendar

We turn over a page of the calendar which the past month is printed on. We tear the past pages and throw them away. It feels like the time passes and disappears forever even though it is deeply connected to to the present. This calender is about time. The relationship between past and present. The part of last month remains. As we tear each page, the remaining scrap connects to the other months. The whole picture shows the floating of time. One leaf beautifully changes its color according to seasonal changes.

Dimensions: 12 x 19 "

www.kankyo-d.co.jp

2008 - Proverbio in Luce
2009 - Entre Escena y Cielo
2010 - Days of White and Traces

Designer: Sachiko Murakami

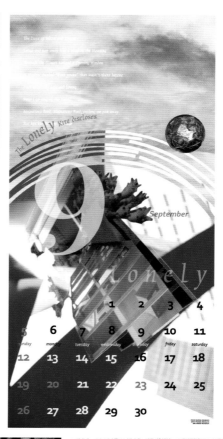

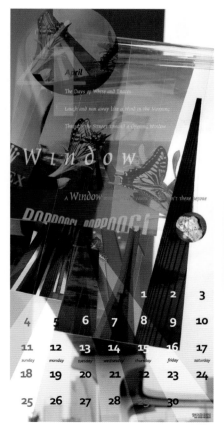

sait alanyali

www.saitalanyali.com

CD Calendar

A lot of people have CDs and DVDs around them. Why not use them as calendars, I thought, and here's the cd calendar! You can write, doodle, make small notes or whatever for each and every day. You can archive the things you did that day, digitally and by hand.

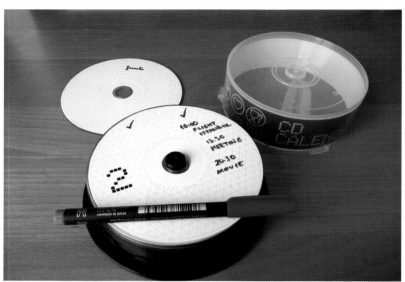

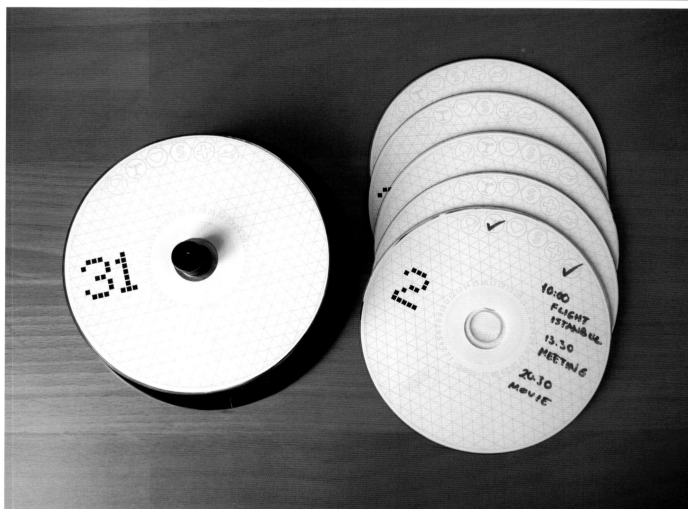

Manufacturer: ABR (www.abrproduccion.com)

Dayboard

The calendar is the result of our attempt to give the user more freedom to arrange their time the way they see fit. Not force all activities into a single square. The calendar consists of a metal backboard and 432 injection moulded ABS pieces. 366 of the pieces are for the days, 14 are white marked with the names of the days (mon, tue, wed..) and then there are 52 white ones with the numbers 1-52 representing the week numbers. These pieces are held on the backboard using magnets so they can be arranged exactly as the user wishes. The magnets can also be used to hold theater tickets, shopping lists or pictures of friends and family.

Dimensions: 100 x 100 x 5 cm

www.behance.net/SimonJoker

The birth of the Universe

This calendar about the Creation of the Universe was a degree project. It is a kind of graphic research, cognition with the help of graphic images. In fact, scientists still don't know how the Universe was born. They have some suppositions and different theories, but no one knows an exact answer. Before creating this project I read a lot of scientific works about outer space, but soon understood that our knowledge about it is equal to zero. That's why I decided just to imagine and to feel, how it may have happened and then I graphically depicted my feelings in images.

01январь02январь03январь04январь05январь06январь07январь08январь09янв
арь10январь11январь12январь13январь14январь15м16январь17январь18янва
рь19январь20январь21январь22январь23январь24январь25январь26январь27я
нварь28январь29январь30январь31январь01февраль02февраль03февраль04ф
евраль05февраль06февраль07февраль08февраль09февраль10февраль11февр
аль12февраль13февраль14февраль15февраль16февраль17февраль18февраль
19февраль20февраль22февраль23февраль24февраль25февраль26февраль27
февраль28февраль29февраль01март02март03март04март05март06март07м
арт08март09март10март11март12март13март14март15март16март17март1
8март19март20март21март22март23март24м25март26март27март28март29
март30март31март01апрель02апрель03апрель04апрель05апрель06апрель07
апрель08апрель09апрель10апрель11апрель12апрель13апрель14апрель15апр
ель16апрель17апрель18апрель19апрель20апрель21апрель22апрель23апрель
24апрель25апрель26апрель27апрель28апрель29апрель30апрель01май02май
03май04май05май06май07м̲а̲й̲ ̲ ̲ ̲ ̲ ̲ ̲ ̲ ̲ ̲ ̲11май12май13май14май1
5май16май17май18май19̲ ̲ ̲ ̲ ̲ ̲ ̲ ̲ ̲ ̲май24май25май26май27
май28май29май30май3̲ ̲ ̲ ̲ ̲ ̲ ̲ ̲июнь05июнь06июнь07и
юнь08июнь09июнь10и̲ ̲ ̲ ̲ ̲ ̲ ̲ ̲июнь16июнь17июнь1
8июнь19июнь20июнь2̲ ̲ ̲ ̲ ̲ ̲ ̲26июнь27июнь28ию
нь29июнь30июнь01и̲ ̲ ̲ ̲ ̲07июль08июль09июл
ь10июль11v12июль1̲ ̲ ̲ ̲ ̲18июль19июль20июль
21июль22июль23июл̲ ̲ ̲ ̲ ̲29июль30июль31ию
ль01августа02августа̲ ̲ ̲ ̲густа07августа08августа
та09августа10августа̲ ̲ ̲густа15августа16авгус
та17августа18август̲19̲ ̲ ̲ ̲ ̲23августа24августа25а
вгуста26августа27августа̲2̲ ̲ ̲ ̲ ̲ ̲густа31августа01сентябрь02
сентябрь03сентябрь04сентябрь̲ ̲ ̲ ̲07сентябрь08сентябрь09сентябр
ь10сентябрь11сентябрь12сентябрь13сентябрь14сентябрь15сентябрь16сентябр
ь17сентябрь18сентябрь19сентябрь20сентябрь21сентябрь22сентябрь23сентябр
ь24сентябрь25сентябрь26сентябрь27сентябрь28сентябрь29сентябрь30сентябр
ь01октябрь02октябрь03октябрь04октябрь05октябрь06октябрь07октябрь08октя
брь09октябрь10октябрь11октябрь12октябрь13октябрь14октябрь15октябрь16ок
тябрь17октябрь18октябрь19октябрь20октябрь21октябрь22октябрь23октябрь24
октябрь25октябрь26октябрь27октябрь28октябрь29октябрь30октябрь31октябрь
01ноябрь02ноябрь03ноябрь04ноябрь05ноябрь06ноябрь07ноябрь08ноябрь09н
оябрь10ноябрь11ноябрь12ноябрь13ноябрь14ноябрь15ноябрь16ноябрь17нояб
рь18ноябрь19ноябрь20ноябрь21ноябрь22ноябрь23ноябрь24ноябрь25ноябрь2
6ноябрь27ноябрь28ноябрь29ноябрь30ноябрь01декабрь02декабрь03декабрь0
4декабрь05декабрь06декабрь07декабрь08декабрь09декабрь10декабрь11дек
абрь12декабрь13декабрь14декабрь15декабрь16декабрь17декабрь19декабрь
20декабрь22декабрь23декабрь24декабрь25декабрь26декабрь27декабрь28де
кабрь29декабрь30декабрь31декабрь

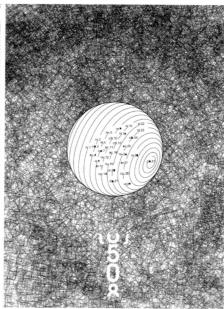

susanna hertrich

www.susannahertrich.com

Chrono-Shredder

The machine as performer. Chrono-Shredder is a poetic time-object that reminds us of the volatility of the »now«. As a hybrid object with functions similar to those of a calendar and a clock, it shreds every single day in realtime. All that time that is irrevisibly lost gets a tangible existence in form of shredded paper. As time passes by, the tattered remains of the past pile up under the device. Chrono-Shredder's final version is currently under development, with dimensions roughly about 500 mm in height, 400 mm in width and 250 mm in depth. It comes in a powder-coated metal casing and features two printed calendar rolls of about 45m in length to cover a whole year. The release of a strictlly limited edition is planned for fall 2010.

This Year 2008, This Year 2009, This Year 2010

Hard to Read Calendar 2010

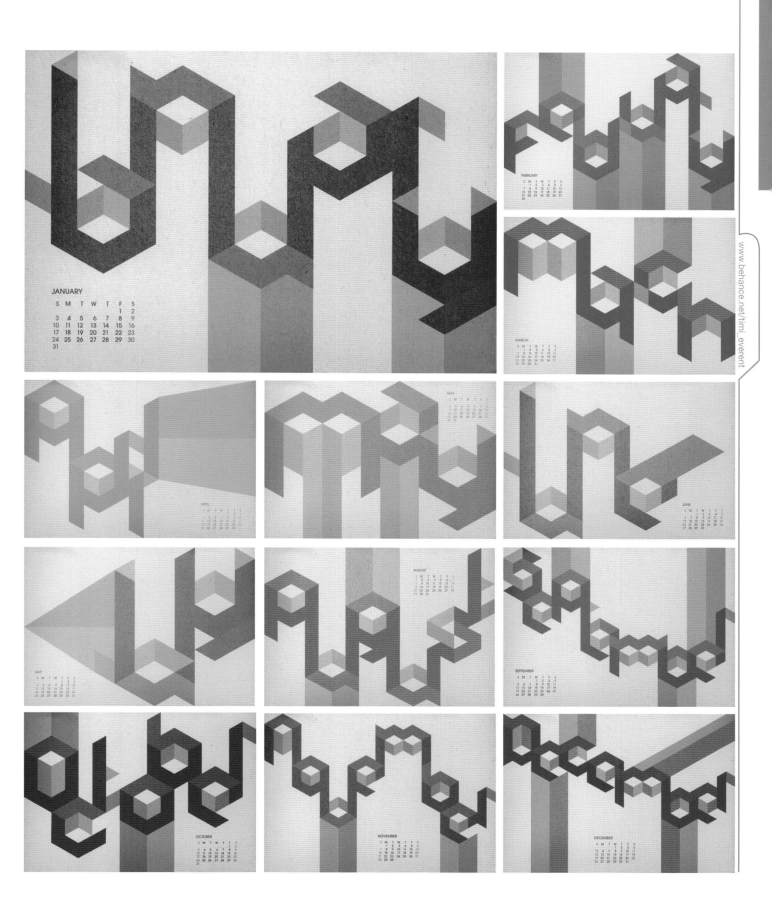

Flip Calendar Book

A student calendar that starts in the fall and ends in the summer. The deciduous tree is a methaphore for student work - it starts as a "tabula rasa", in the process it gains leaves and at the end of the year it the fruits of its work are ready for harvesting.

Dimensions: 120 x 120 mm (14 mm thick)

Client: Youth service Kranj
Copywriters: Teja Kleč & Tomato Košir
Art direction & design: Tomato Košir
Printed by: Grafex

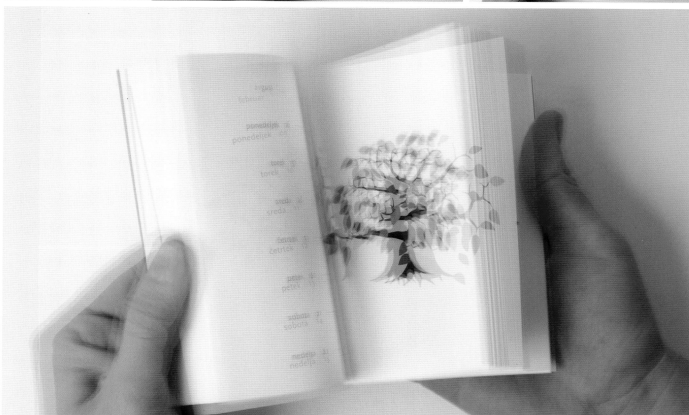

"Live With.." Calendar (2009)

This calendar has been produced with the desire to place the highest priority on preserving the environment and learning to live in harmony with nature. This calendar is printed by "Kareid" inks to help save energy. In addition special printing technology is used to make it a fun experience to touch the illustrations and view them from different angles.

Dimensions: 465 x 472 mm

Client: Toyo Ink Mfg. Co Ltd
Creative Director: Takehiko Watanabe
Art Director: Masahiro Aoyag
Illustration: U.G. Sato (Design Farm)
Design: U.G. Sato, Kohei Sakamoto
Printing: Toppan Printing Co Ltd

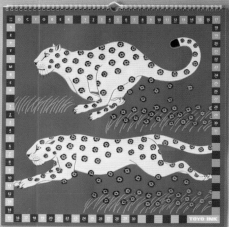

Design / Illustration: U.G. Sato
Printing: Assidu Planning Co Ltd

Mt. Fuji (2008, 2009, 2010 Design Farm Calendar)

Mt. Fuji is a very beautiful and famous Mountain in Japan. It has been drawn by many famous painters through history. Above all, Hokusai 36 views of Mt. Fuji is a very famous wood print. Inspiring his 36 views, U.G. Sato drew 36 different views of Mt. Fuji for Calendars in 2008, 2009, 2010. He expressed the figure of Mt. Fuji from a modern viewpoint with humour, esprit and satire.

Dimensions: 297 x 594 mm

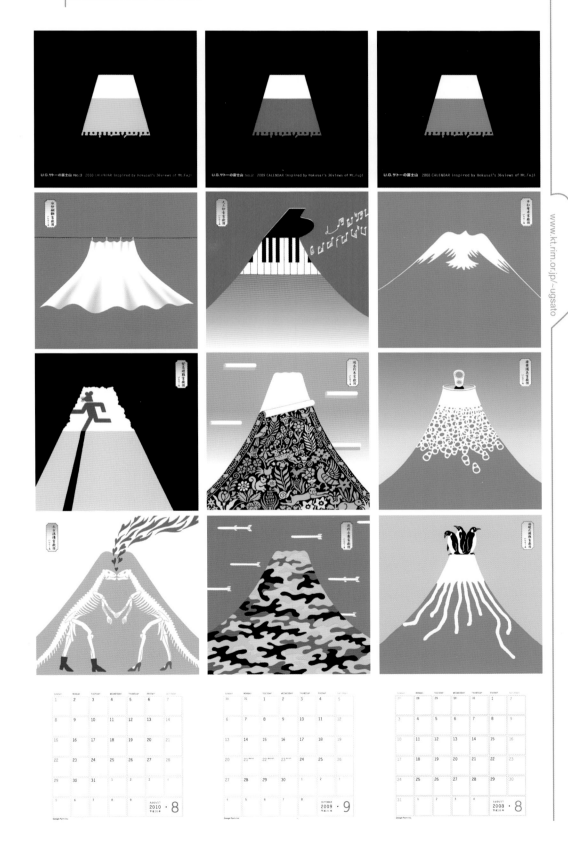

Typographic Bodoni Calendar

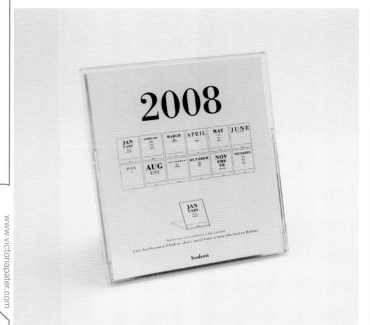

Memory Calendar

The concept behind the memory calendar was to create a calendar that reflected various memories or the various meaning of memories while at the same time functioning as a regular calendar. The process involved using branches, photographic film, duct tape, and Plexiglas. Apart from this the only software used was Photoshop. The project was entirely put together by hand and each Plexiglas is 3in X 3in.

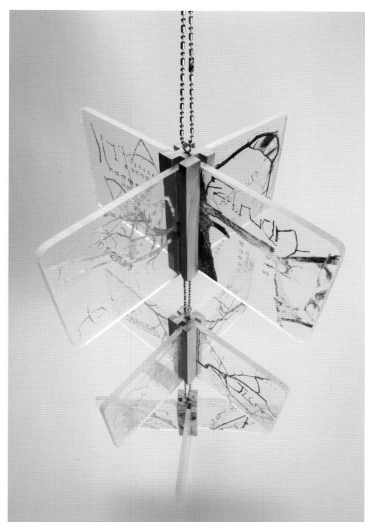

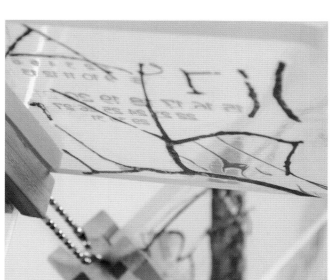

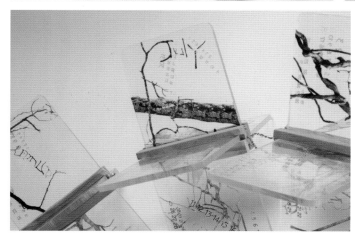

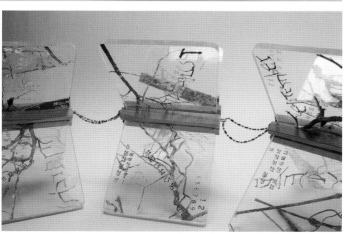

aleksander shevchuk

www.shevchuk.eyelevation.ru

The calendar has 6 pop-up figures. A rigid cover with black metallic logos on each side. There are page magnets so that it can hold the page in an upright position. The calendar's slogan was translated from Russian as: Full scale print. It lays down the principle of a pop-up book. Fluor Pantone was also used for more "juice". Realized in 4 fluor pantones (801c, 802c, 803c, 806c) and stamping black foil.

Dimensions: 33 x 18", 3-4 Kg

Client: Printing House Typography 21

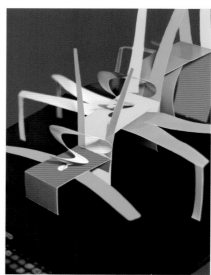

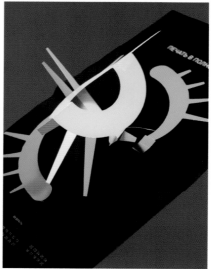

Client: Printing House Typography 21

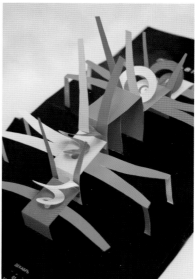

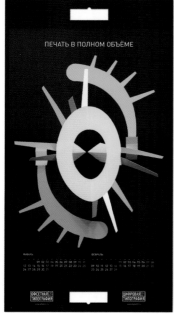
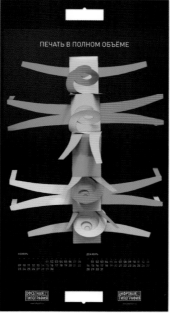
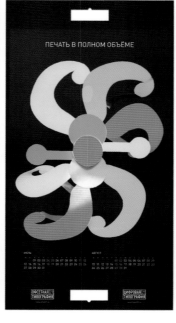
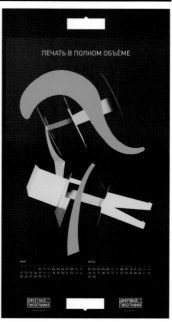

andy v mordovtsev

Sea Port of Saint-Petersburg

Client: JSC "Sea Port of Saint-Petersburg"

Composition of Direct Mail: Kit Build 3D puzzle, tea strainer, sugar cane. A person who receives a gift from direct mail has the chance to have a good time assembling the 3D puzzle and a cup of tea. This unique 3D calendar will decorate the wall throughout the year.

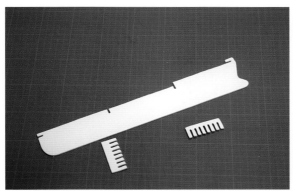
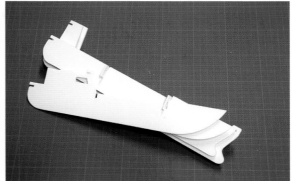
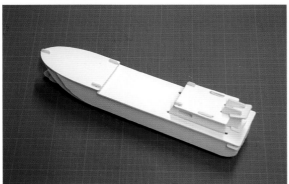

Box It - 2010 Calendar

Client: Jingpin Paper

When days and weeks become merely numbers, what meaning does the future hold for us? "Box It" takes the form of a gift box, inside there are 4 additional mini boxes, the faces of each use various typefaces to create an interesting navigation experience for the user. The mini boxes can also be unfolded and re-folded inside out to become gift boxes to pass on your blessings of the year. May surprises never end in your 2010.

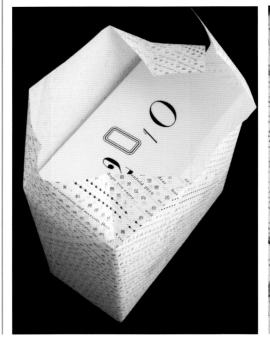

Client: Antalis Paper, Pékin

THINK RE...

Think, contemplate, ponder; Re, again, repeat. Recycle, circulate; reuse, use again; reduce, deduct; retro, in fashion again; reborn, live again; redesign, design again. THINK RE… is an annual calendar for Antalis Paper, Beijing and a reference manual on the topic of paper reuse. Paper exists in every aspect of our life - in the form of a notebook, a leaflet, a stack of old newspapers, an outdated poster, maybe you are just about to throw it away. It could have been given a brand new life. Think about the calendar fashion in the 80s, when you turned your most beloved old calendar into blinds, wallets or book cover. In a time where there was a shortage of materials, fashion naturally extended the life of paper, and brought life unlimited joy. THINK RE… is not a retro, trend-following act, but an awakening of the memories of reuse. Pick up waste paper, think again, make its life continue. Give yourself one more chance to choose, give paper one more life; give the earth one more breath.

Dimensions: 310 x 470 mm, 62 Pages, 1000 Copies

lava (orientationlab)

www.orientationlab.com

Spinhex Printers selected LAVA (OrientationLab) to design their annual desktop calendar. The calendar was made to keep on giving throughout the year: each month is an envelope containing either a mask, chess-set or another small surprise. The tactile aspect of this calendar is important: humble materials become interesting through printing and die-cuts. The monthly envelopes reveal 12 little gifts, objects made out of paper and cardboard. Graphics and typography shows and interesting way to connect eastern and western visual cultures.

Client: Spinhex & industry
Art Director: Anne Miltenburg
Designer: Reza Abedini

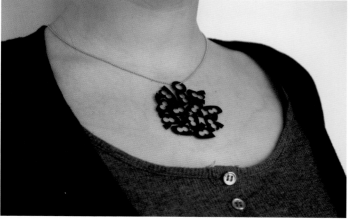

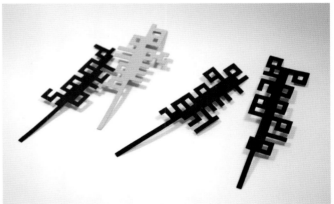

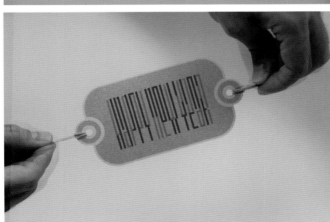

point blank design ltd

www.pointblank.com.hk

Playing Cards - Hundred Thousand Ways

Being CURIOUS, PLAYFUL and QUESTIONING are the core values of creativity. These essential elements were combined in this card game design on Antalis Curious paper.

Client: Antalis (HK) Ltd
Designer: Times Pang, Jack Wong

www.qaaimgood.netii.net

The concept behind the calendar came from studying a wide array of Italian design mixed with the idea of time. Time is a very interesting subject, especially in how to portray it visually. The original idea for the calendar came from trying to make a modernize sundial that followed how a clock works going clockwise. Instead it morphed into something more economical to be more of service to the working class. The project itself expanded from a class assignment in my junior year at Memphis College of Art, where we were given the task to build a gift for graduating seniors in the design program. I simply took it further and implemented my own flavor to the assignment to help produce the calendar. I am now gearing up to have these manufactured so they can be purchased worldwide.

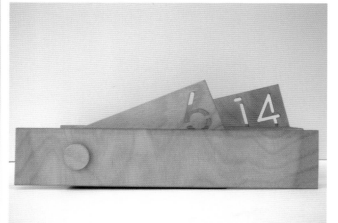

www.thought.co.jp

Corrugated Cardboard Box Calendar

I added a function called "the calendar" to "the cardboard box" which was to reuse resources. It plays 2 roles just by printing a calendar on a box. You could know the date when you used the box if you mark it on a date. Because you can set storing days on a delivery date and the arrival day, the use of the corrugated cardboard is spread. And also you can distinguish the thing of how many years at first sight by displaying of big size number. The letters were printed in a fluorescent color making it easy to see in a dark place. A rise in the utility value by adding design to common household goods.

Art Direction / Design: Souichi Ozawa
Design: Yuma Higuchi

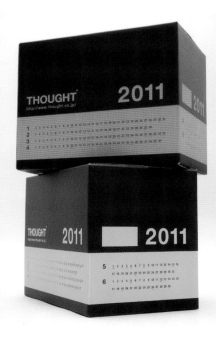

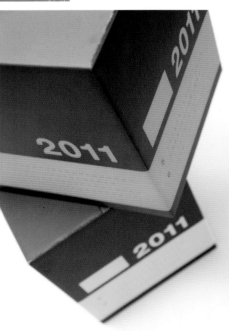

Dorogaya Magnetic Calendar (2007)

Eternal, easily customized magnetic calendar. With, even, a 32nd day in each month just in case. Months' names abbreviated to 3 letters. Chips can be placed one over another. The special appeal of this calendar are the special chips, like "Deadline", "Arrival", "Departure", five "Drink Day" and one "Don't Drink Day". Materials & techniques involved: Color printing on magnet badges.

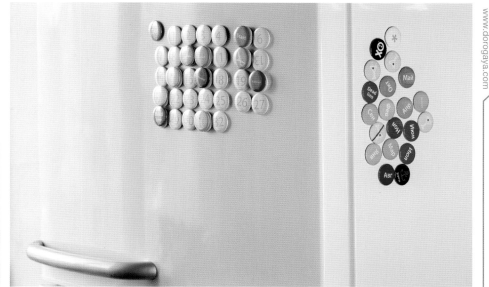

Ink Me Stencil Calendar (2009)

Client; Ink Systems is young aggressive company; they deal with lots of ink for printing systems. So, we were looking for unusual aggressive ink calendar. Our solution is stencil set with all necessary ingredients. We call it INK ME. Calendar pack contains: cyan, magenta and yellow spray inks, 3 stencil layers, stickers with numbers, several types of 50/70 paper (including old wallpaper) and big craft paper sheet to work on it. You get custom 50/70 poster calendar at the end of a process. And of course you can use this stencils not only on paper from our pack. Materials & techniques involved: 3 stencils, 3 paint cans, sticker and wallpapers

Target Practice (2011)

The client, GfK, is an international market research organization. For the Ukrainian division of GfK, we have created an interactive calendar. Packed in a matt black wooden box. Calendar page illustrations are diagrams, formed as shooting targets. The interactive part of this calendar are 2 sets of dart arrows (3 cyan and 3 magenta colored, representing male and female auditory). So, you can literally hit the target group. Materials & techniques involved: Dartboard, 2 sets of dart arrows, offset printing.

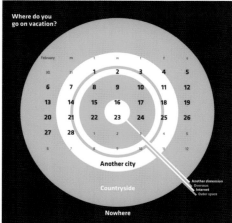

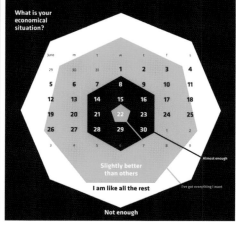

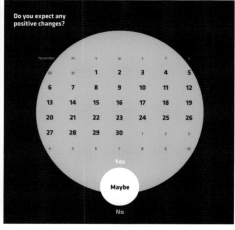

Calendar 2009

A one-of-a-kind promotional calendar designed as a give-away gift for the year 2009. It contains
a series of coasters, which double as a calendar and a snapshot of our portfolio from the previous
year. The box also boasts some delightfully scented Lebanese hand-made soaps, a witty reminder
to keep the scent of Lebanon around with you, on your desk, in your home!

Dimensions: 10.5 x 10.5 x 3.5 cm

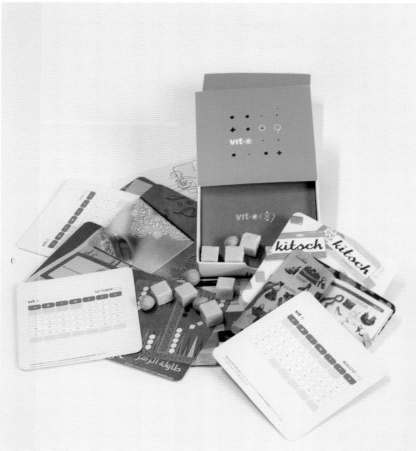

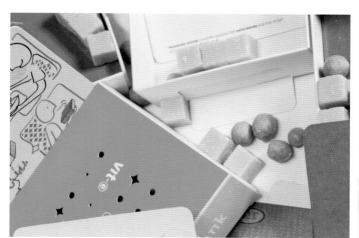

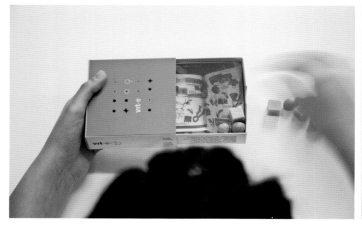

McDonald's Calendar 365

At the end of the year, McDonald's asked us to develop an idea that shows their appreciation for their franchisees and business partners. The idea was to create a memorable gift that portrayed the franchisor McDonald's in a positive way reflecting the brand values. Shortly said: straight forward enthusiasm. We captured one magical moment of the McDonald's experience – the build-up of anticipation for the food that occurs when taking a napkin just before eating – and transported this feeling to business partners' offices 365 times a year by using a napkin dispenser which serves as a tear-off calender. The German phrase, "Einen Guten!", is a short form of, "enjoy your meal" as well as, "have a good day". There were many spontaneous and happy responses – and up to now, successful cooperation in the new year.

Client: McDonald's Germany Inc
Creative Director: Peter Hirrlinger, Zeljko Pezely
Art Director: Florian Binder
Copywriter: Christoph Gaehwiler
Agency Producer: Carsten Horn, Petra Remmling
Account: Carina Eickmann
CMO McDonald's: James Woodbridge

Designer: Petra Cvelbar

Jezero / The Lake

This calendar is made up of picture excerpts from Ziga Koritnik's book of black and white photographic impressions which was released in 2009. It is the result of 4 years working in all periods of the year. Lake Bohinj in Slovenia is the place that he is connected to and regulary visiting since his childhood. Pictures were made on digital format, manipulated on computer in a film way, softly warm toned.

Dimensions: 480 x 360 mm, 170g/m2, Matt lacquered.

www.lifelounge.com

Some Type of Wonderful

The basic concept of htis calendar is that each year we invite 12 of our favourite designers, artists and typographers to respond to a typographic design brief that relates to a specific month and what that month means to them.

Curated / Produced: Lifelounge
Designers:
Cover by: Luke Lucas
June: Theo Gennitsakis
November: Steve Powers
August: Pablo Alfieri
October: Niels Shoe Meulman
March: Jesse Hora

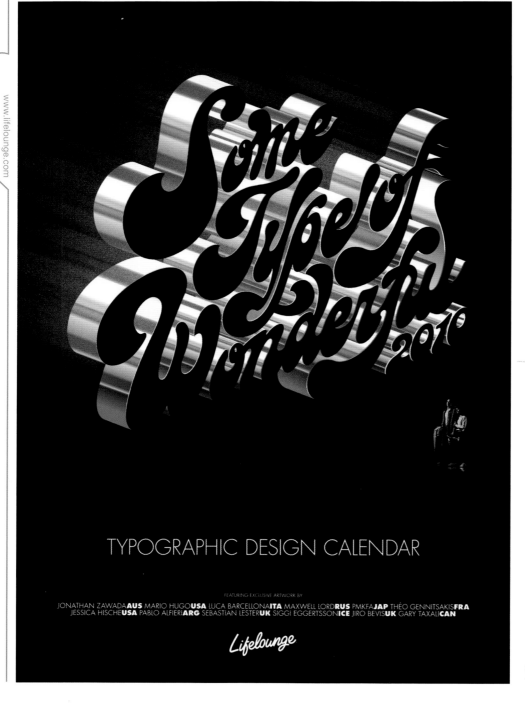

MARCH
JESSE HORA

SUN MON TUE WED THU FRI SAT SUN MON TUE WED THU FRI SAT SUN MON TUE WED THU FRI SAT SUN MON TUE WED THU FRI SAT SUN MON TUE
1 2 3 4 5 6 7 8 9 10 11 12 13 14 15 16 17 18 19 20 21 22 23 24 25 26 27 28 29 30 31

Lifelounge

JUNE

NOVEMBER

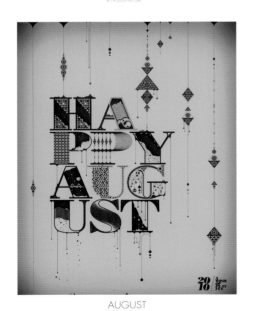

AUGUST

FEBRUARY

OCTOBER

zdenko bracevac design

www.zbracevac.com

Calendar 2006

Client: AKRAPOVIC Exhaust System Tehnology
(Ljubljana Slovenia)
Ad, Concept / Design: Zdenko Bracevac
Photography: Blaz Zupancic
Printing on Polypropylene : G Plast

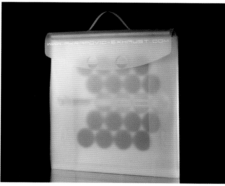

Self Promotional Calendar

Since ancient times, people have been passing on information in various ways. The calendar, which informs us of dates by numbers, can also be considered one such means. This calendar, in which I attempted to inform dates in 12 different ways, is sure to stimulate the intellectual curiosity of a wide range of generations. Additionally, I limited the material to only paper and made it possible to use either as a wall calendar or a desk calendar.

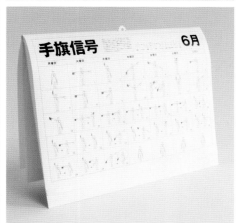

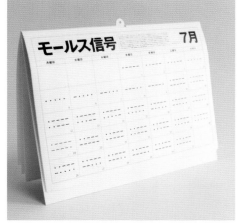

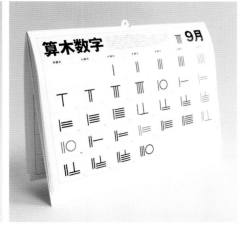

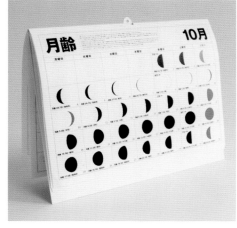

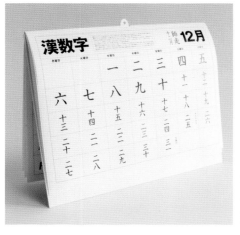

These are a series of compact desk calendars made to fit in tight areas of your daily life. Each of them can be folded into pleats (accordion fold) , so that you can enjoy arranging it in many ways.

a life, variously Happy Life

The theme of this work is ecology and that concept is "a life, variously HAPPY LIFE". Every day, you bend the date of that day of this calendar before going to sleep. And you can reconfirm the daily importance which is often forgot carelessly. I used YUPO (it is the 100% recyclable, waterproof, tree-free Synthetic Paper) for the material of this calendar. At the end of the year, you can use this calendar as a drainer of kitchen garbage. every month is expressed by a different color.

Dimensions: 728mm x 1030mm

2011

SUN	MON	TUE	WED	THU	FRI	SAT																																

🌲🌲🌲🌲🌲🌲🌲 1 2 3 4 5 6 7 8 9 10 11 12 13 14 15 16 17 18 19 20 21 22 23 24 25 26 27 28 29 30 31

🌲🌲 1 2 3 4 5 6 7 8 9 10 11 12 13 14 15 16 17 18 19 20 21 22 23 24 25 26 27 28 🌲🌲🌲🌲🌲🌲

🌲🌲 1 2 3 4 5 6 7 8 9 10 11 12 13 14 15 16 17 18 19 20 21 22 23 24 25 26 27 28 29 30 31 🌲🌲🌲🌲

🌲🌲🌲🌲🌲🌲 1 2 3 4 5 6 7 8 9 10 11 12 13 14 15 16 17 18 19 20 21 22 23 24 25 26 27 28 29 30 🌲🌲

1 2 3 4 5 6 7 8 9 10 11 12 13 14 15 16 17 18 19 20 21 22 23 24 25 26 27 28 29 30 31 🌲🌲🌲🌲🌲🌲

🌲🌲🌲 1 2 3 4 5 6 7 8 9 10 11 12 13 14 15 16 17 18 19 20 21 22 23 24 25 26 27 28 29 30 🌲🌲🌲🌲

🌲🌲🌲🌲 1 2 3 4 5 6 7 8 9 10 11 12 13 14 15 16 17 18 19 20 21 22 23 24 25 26 27 28 29 30 31 🌲

🌲 1 2 3 4 5 6 7 8 9 10 11 12 13 14 15 16 17 18 19 20 21 22 23 24 25 26 27 28 29 30 31 🌲🌲🌲🌲

🌲🌲🌲🌲 1 2 3 4 5 6 7 8 9 10 11 12 13 14 15 16 17 18 19 20 21 22 23 24 25 26 27 28 29 30 🌲🌲🌲

🌲🌲🌲🌲🌲🌲 1 2 3 4 5 6 7 8 9 10 11 12 13 14 15 16 17 18 19 20 21 22 23 24 25 26 27 28 29 30 31

🌲🌲🌲 1 2 3 4 5 6 7 8 9 10 11 12 13 14 15 16 17 18 19 20 21 22 23 24 25 26 27 28 29 30 🌲🌲🌲🌲

🌲🌲🌲🌲 1 2 3 4 5 6 7 8 9 10 11 12 13 14 15 16 17 18 19 20 21 22 23 24 25 26 27 28 29 30 31 🌲🌲

🌲 You'd like to make the incision to the dotted line on the day and fold it before it sleeps.   🌲 When you finished using the calendar, you cut this. And, you can use this as a drainer of garbage.

natsuko ezura

Braille Calendar

The design of the calendar is based on a flower theme which can be enjoyed by all people with and without vision impairments. For those with vision, I would like them to enjoy the calendar not simply as a source of information, but more so as an interior decor with a multitude of expressions and colors through the special silk screen print and mirror surfaces. For those with vision disabilities, instead of the work being a simple Braille calendar, I would like them to directly feel the raised floral silk print to feel the diverse expressions of flowers of each season. I have created this work to underline the message that design and its corresponding meanings can be enjoyed by all people with varying sensory abilities. I would hence like people with regular vision to enjoy the work through observing its spatial compositions while those with vision impairments can enjoy the same messages through the direct "feeling" of the surfaces.

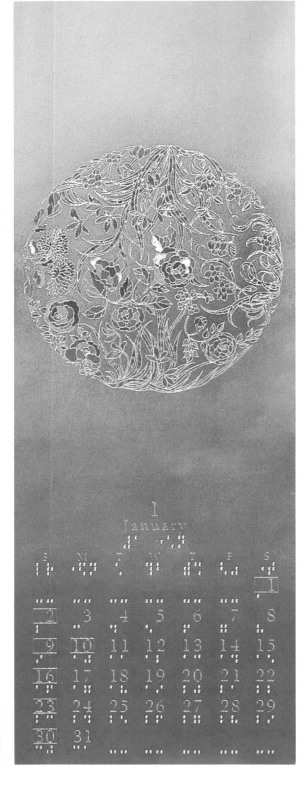

Urban Calendar

The skyscraper was developed because real estate in the city was becoming more and more expensive. In an urban area where land is limited and real estate is valuable, we build up (as it turns out this is a very "Green" way to build). Just like the city, the modern day desk has a limited amount of valuable real estate. With the URBAN CALENDAR you get the entire year in a very small footprint, 8 square inches. The URBAN CALENDAR has and elegant elliptical foot print that is 4" x 2.5" and rises to a height of just under 24" for its 53 stories (weeks).

Designer: boB
Photography: Brandon Stengel
(www.farmkidstudios.com)

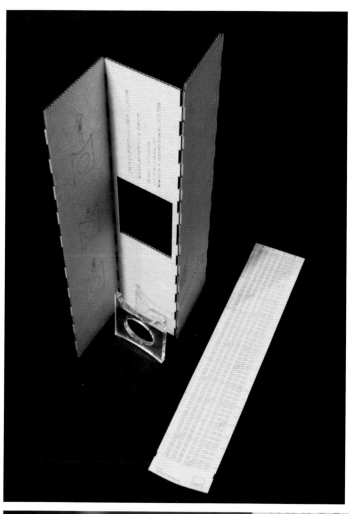

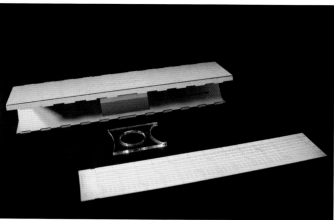

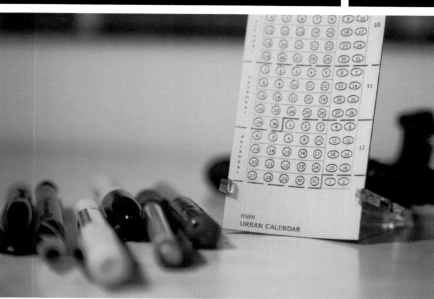

mini
URBAN CALENDAR

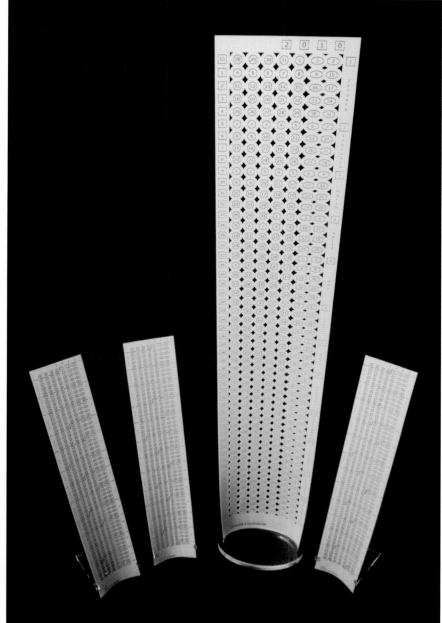

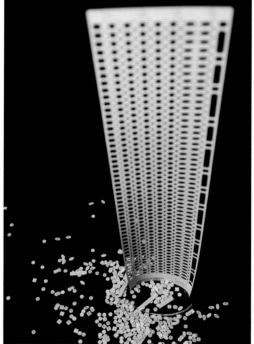

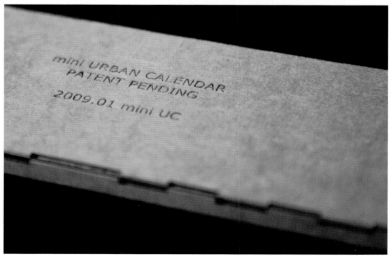

www.dfeijoo.com

MSF 2008

Main activities of MSF during 2006. Each month is illustrated with a number that represent the total cases treated in relation with a humanity cause.

Dimensions: 105 x 74.25 mm + base

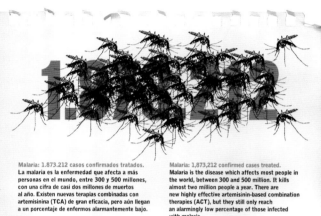

Malaria: 1.873.212 casos confirmados tratados.
La malaria es la enfermedad que afecta a más personas en el mundo, entre 300 y 500 millones, con una cifra de casi dos millones de muertos al año. Existen nuevas terapias combinadas con artemisinina (TCA) de gran eficacia, pero aún llegan a un porcentaje de enfermos alarmantemente bajo.

Malaria: 1,873,212 confirmed cases treated.
Malaria is the disease which affects most people in the world, between 300 and 500 million. It kills almost two million people a year. There are new highly effective artemisinin-based combination therapies (ACT), but they still only reach an alarmingly low percentage of those infected with malaria.

Cólera: 88.732 pacientes admitidos en centros de tratamiento del cólera o tratados con soluciones de rehidratación oral.
Decenas de miles de personas sufren cada año en África el azote del cólera, a veces en zonas donde ni siquiera es endémico, otras veces en nuevos escenarios como las abigarradas periferias de las grandes ciudades, propagándose siempre con una rapidez fulminante.

Cholera: 88,732 patients admitted to cholera treatment centres or treated with oral rehydration solution.
Every year tens of thousands of people in Africa suffer the scourge of cholera, sometimes in areas which are not even endemic, other times in new settings like the heterogeneous outskirts of big cities, the disease always spreading at great speed.

Cirugía: 64.416 intervenciones quirúrgicas; 9.325 operaciones en situación de conflicto.
Casi el 60% de los proyectos de MSF tienen por escenario países en conflicto, post-conflicto o inestables, donde se impone la cirugía de guerra. Pero en el 40% restante, la urgencia también existe para pacientes cuya vida depende de una operación demasiado cara o que ni siquiera se practica por falta de medios y personal.

Surgery: 64,416 surgical operations; 9,325 operations in conflict settings.
Almost 60% of MSF projects take place in conflict, post-conflict, or unstable zones where war surgery is necessary. In the remaining 40% there is also urgent need however as there are patients whose lives depend on operations that are too expensive or that can not be performed due to lack of means and staff.

Salud mental: 93.066 personas atendidas en sesiones individuales; 12.665 participantes en sesiones de grupo.
Mashkul: expresión usada en **Darfur** para "la profunda preocupación de las mentes y los corazones por lo que pasó y lo que pasará". En contextos de conflicto, catástrofes naturales, emergencias nutricionales o epidemias, la atención psicológica y psicosocial es parte integral de la acción humanitaria.

Mental health: 93,066 individual consultations; 12,665 participants in group sessions.
Mashkul: expression used in **Darfur** for "the profound concern of minds and hearts for what happened and what will happen". In conflicts, natural catastrophes, nutritional emergencies or epidemics, psychological and psychosocial care are a fundamental part of humanitarian aid.

Violencia sexual: 11.126 casos atendidos por todo tipo de violencia sexual.
La violencia sexual, una de las más brutales formas de violencia sufridas por los civiles en los conflictos, se ha convertido en un arma más de guerra. Sus consecuencias médicas y psicológicas –agravadas por la amenaza del sida– pueden ser devastadoras para la víctima.

Sexual violence: 11,126 cases of sexual violence treated.
Sexual violence, one of the most brutal forms of violence suffered by civilians during conflicts, has become yet another weapon of war. Its medical and psychological consequences –exacerbated by the threat of Aids– can be devastating for the victims.

MSF2007

Dimensions: 105 x 74.25 mm + base

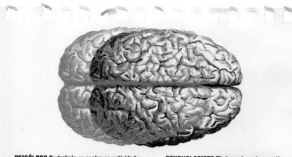

PSICÓLOGO Su trabajo se centra en actividades de salud mental y apoyo psicosocial a las poblaciones en contextos de conflicto, violencia, catástrofes naturales, etc. Sus principales funciones son la atención clínica directa, actividades preventivas, capacitación de personal y de líderes comunitarios, y coordinación de las actividades de salud mental de los proyectos.

PSYCHOLOGISTS Their work centres on the provision of mental healthcare and psycho-social support to populations who have been victims of conflict, violence, natural catastrophes, etc. Their main functions are direct clinical care, preventive activities, the provision of training to staff and community leaders, and the coordination of mental health activities.

MSF 2007

www.msf.es

MEDICOS SIN FRONTERAS

OTROS ESPECIALISTAS
Para proyectos concretos, necesitamos: nutricionistas, cirujanos, anestesistas, ginecólogos o epidemiólogos.

OTHER SPECIALISTS
Nutritionists, surgeons, anaesthetists, gynaecologists and epidemiologists are needed for specific projects.

MATRONA Lleva a cabo actividades relacionadas con la salud materno infantil y reproductiva. Participa en la identificación de necesidades, análisis epidemiológicos y supervisión de protocolos. Supervisa y forma al personal sanitario, además de las actividades propias que conlleva la función de matrona en clínicas, maternidades o centros de salud, a menudo en zonas rurales.

MIDWIVES They are in charge of activities regarding mother-child healthcare and reproductive health. They participate in the identification of needs, they carry out epidemiological analyses and they oversee protocols. They also supervise and train healthcare staff in addition to providing midwife support at clinics, maternity wards and health centres, often in rural areas.

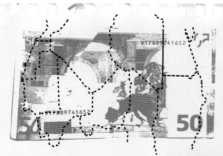

ADMINISTRADOR / FINANCIERO Se ocupa de la contabilidad, el control presupuestario, la elaboración de informes y propuestas financieras, así como de la supervisión de personal administrativo local, gestión de plantilla, elaboración de contratos laborales, gestión de impuestos y el pago de los salarios.

ADMINISTRATORS / FINANCIAL CONTROLLERS They are responsible for accounting, budget supervision, the compiling of financial reports and proposals, as well as the supervision of local administrative personnel, staff management, the drawing up of work contracts, tax management and the payment of salaries.

TÉCNICO EN INFORMACIÓN, EDUCACIÓN Y COMUNICACIÓN (IEC) Se encarga de informar y sensibilizar a la comunidad sobre temas de salud (violencia sexual, VIH/sida, salud sexual y reproductiva, estigmatización, higiene...) en un proyecto determinado. Forma al personal sanitario en metodologías educativas y coordina la implementación de las actividades de IEC con las instituciones locales, otras contrapartes y los beneficiarios.

INFORMATION, EDUCATION AND COMMUNICATION (IEC) TECHNICIANS Their role is to educate and raise awareness among the community on matters such as health (sexual violence, HIV/AIDS, sexual and reproductive health, stigmatization, hygiene, etc.) on specific projects. They train healthcare staff in educative methodologies and coordinate IEC activities with local institutions, counterparts, and the populations.

Engaged: The Calendar of W.C. Celebration

Taking the humour of toilet graffiti into the comfort of your own lavatory, this is a flushable calendar for your daily toilet visit. The inspiration here is to integrate a daily activity with the opportunity to find out the date. The calendar is comprised of a series of flushable sheets that exhibit a different photograph / illustration every day of the year, each from a public toilet with the exact whereabouts marked at the top of each page. The calendar directs you to a website that showcases a gallery guide to all the exhibits around the world so one could visit the original artworks in person.

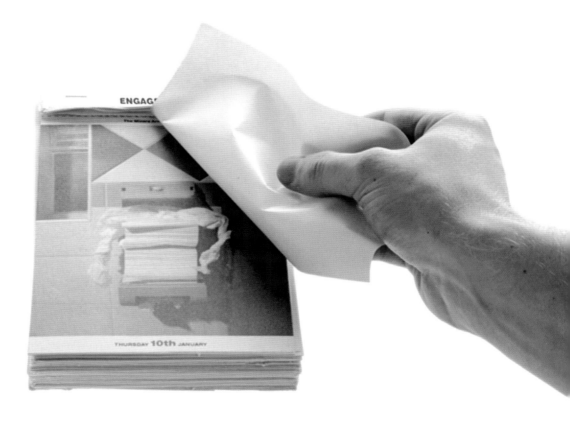

Pierre Victoire, York

SATURDAY **5th** JANUARY

Dog and Gun, Sheffield

THURSDAY **3rd** JANUARY

The Adelphi, Newcastle

FRIDAY **4th** JANUARY

The Woodman, Essex

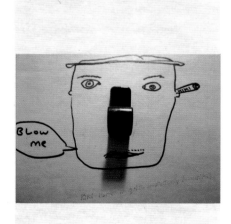

SUNDAY **6th** JANUARY

The Sexey's Arms, Somerset

MONDAY **7th** JANUARY

The Marquis of Lorne, Nottingham

TUESDAY **8th** JANUARY

johann volkmer

www.faltjahr2010.de

A wall calendar which consists of 12 separate A4-sized modules (A3 when open), represented as paper engineered pop-up sculptures. The calendar data is realised by charts and graphs and is individually adapted to fit the shapes of the paper sculptures. Monochrome white paper expresses monthly themes with simple elegance. The Faltjahr 2010 shows what paper is capable of. Check out www.johannvolkmer.de for more work.

Photography: Kristian Barthen

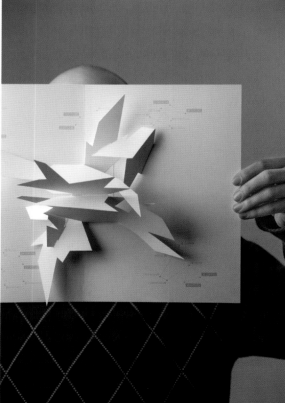

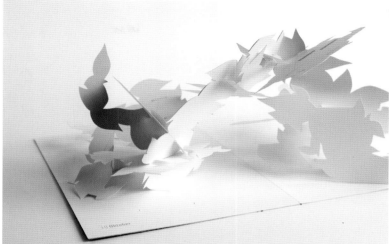

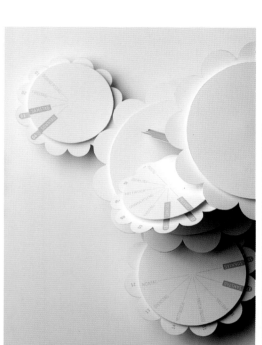

www.kawakong.com

Mr.Clean Calendar 07

Life begins on the other side of despair - Jean-Paul Sartre, wishing you a happy new year.

During the late 2008, our client expressed their concern about the speculated 2009 world economic downfall. Responding to the issue, we came up with a theme about... 'Sometimes things don't turn out the way you want. Don't feel too bad. Something may turn out good for you.'

size: 9cm x 9.3cm. 2 spot colours. Printed on Ivory Card, 230gsm.

Design: Chung and Ming
Client: Mr.Clean
Year: 2009
What they do: Launderette

www.kawakong.com

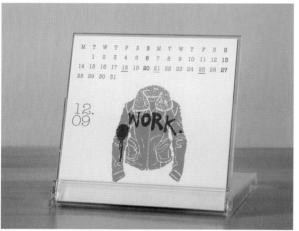

Design: Chung and Ming
Client: Kawakong Designworks
Year: 2007
What they do: Graphic and Identity design.

Kawakong Calendar

The objective of our self promotional calendar design is to introduce the other side of us by featuring our "newly-discovered drawing".

size: 9cm x 9.3cm. 2 spot colours. Printed on Mohawk Superfine Ultra White Eggshell, 216gsm.

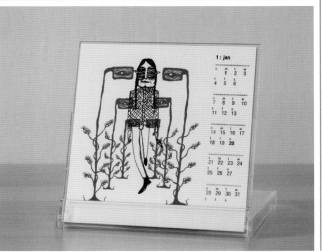

Hummingbirds

Publisher: Gingko Press Inc.
Designer: Benjamin Wolbergs

"The Birds of Manhattan was the first of my large scale street art projects. I painted over 40 hummingbirds in lower Manhattan below fourteenth street. Except in Soho where all the galleries were. Each bird took about 2 hours to complete. It seems difficult to believe now but when the cops or supers caught me I never got in any serious trouble. In fact, once they saw I was painting a hummingbird, almost invariably they'd let me finish." - 1979

May   2011 – 05

mon	tue	wed	thu	fri	sat	sun
						01
02	03	04	05	06	07	08
09	10	11	12	13	14	15
16	17	18	19	20	21	22
23	24	25	26	27	28	29
30	31					

June   2011 – 06

mon	tue	wed	thu	fri	sat	sun
	01	02	03	04	05	
06	07	08	09	10	11	12
13	14	15	16	17	18	19
20	21	22	23	24	25	26
27	28	29	30			

July   2011 – 07

mon	tue	wed	thu	fri	sat	sun
				01	02	03
04	05	06	07	08	09	10
11	12	13	14	15	16	17
18	19	20	21	22	23	24
25	26	27	28	29	30	31

August   2011 – 08

mon	tue	wed	thu	fri	sat	sun
01	02	03	04	05	06	07
08	09	10	11	12	13	14
15	16	17	18	19	20	21
22	23	24	25	26	27	28
29	30	31				

September   2011 – 09

mon	tue	wed	thu	fri	sat	sun
			01	02	03	04
05	06	07	08	09	10	11
12	13	14	15	16	17	18
19	20	21	22	23	24	25
26	27	28	29	30		

October   2011 – 10

mon	tue	wed	thu	fri	sat	sun
					01	02
03	04	05	06	07	08	09
10	11	12	13	14	15	16
17	18	19	20	21	22	23
24	25	26	27	28	29	30
31						

November   2011 – 11

mon	tue	wed	thu	fri	sat	sun
	01	02	03	04	05	06
07	08	09	10	11	12	13
14	15	16	17	18	19	20
21	22	23	24	25	26	27
28	29	30				

December   2011 – 12

mon	tue	wed	thu	fri	sat	sun
			01	02	03	04
05	06	07	08	09	10	11
12	13	14	15	16	17	18
19	20	21	22	23	24	25
26	27	28	29	30	31	

emily okada

www.cargocollective.com/emilyokada

Fill-in-the-blank Calendar

This calendar was made to suit the needs of the average joe American, the suppressed and stifled worker trapped in a cubicle- whoever longs for a touch of art, beauty and rebellion, no matter how small. Simply tear off the days page, and create your own sentence. Fill in the blanks. Keep it private and non-de- structive... or perhaps use it to anonymously leave an inappropriate message on the memo your boss just posted. It doesnt really matter how you fill it in, just be creative. Make someone elses day (and yours) a little more interesting. I was interested in the way that days are all connected (hence the cutouts and connected phrases), but everyone has the choice to change the day however they want.

Colourscan 09

Created as a giveaway item for Colourscan Co (Pte) Ltd., this calendar parodies a Pantone Color Chart. Printed using a unique proprietary technique, the colour chart showcases Colourscan's ability to make accurate color reproductions. The colors in this calendar are a broad reference to the seasonal changes of the Northern Hemisphere. They have been selected according to the colors generally associated with each season – ie, bright colors for spring, greyish hues for winter.

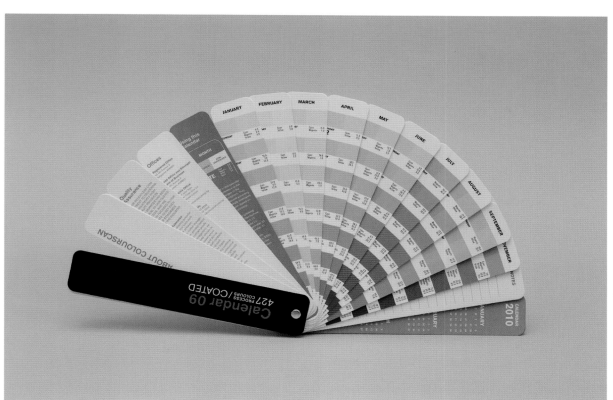

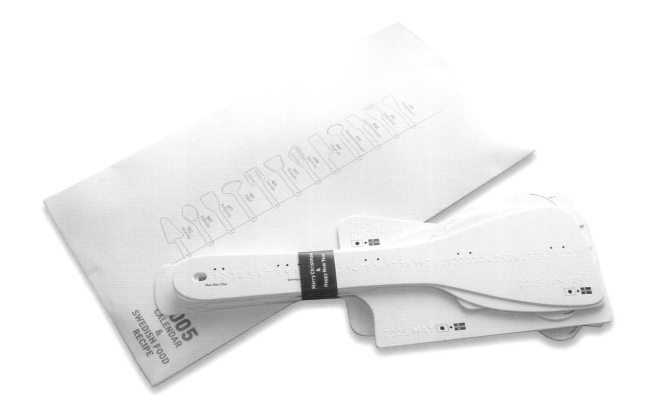

2007
CALENDAR

USE OF THIS CALENDAR.

CALE NDAR

USE A RUBBER BAND
TO KEEP A BOOK OPENED.

©ICHIKUDO PRINTING CO., LTD.

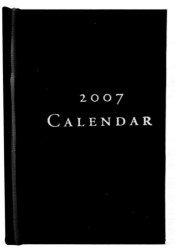

2007

		SUN	MON	TUE	WED	THU	FRI	SAT
		1	2	3	4	5	6	7
		8	9	10	11	12	13	14
		15	16 MARINE DAY	17	18	19	20	21
		22	23	24	25	26	27	28
		29	30	31				

JULY

contents

© Linksbooks
jonqueres, 10, 1-5
08003 barcelona, spain
tel.: +34-93-301-21-99
fax: +34-93-301-00-21
info@linksbooks.net
www.linksbooks.net

published by:
basheer graphic books
block 231, bain street, #04-19
bras basah complex
singapore 180 231
t: (65) 6336 0810
f: (65) 6334 1950
e: abdul@basheegraphic.com
w: www.basheergraphic.com

concept: abdul nasser
curator: euphemia toong
designed by: bigbros workshop
printed by: dami editorial & printing services, china

Acknowledgements

basheer graphic books would like to thank all the designers and studios for their kind consent to publish their works and the photographers who have generously granted the permission to use their images. we would like to show our appreciation to those who have made significant contributions and provided great support. you know who you are – without you, there wouldn't be creative calendars!